"I have twice worked through 2 Corinthians w[ith] commentary and benefited enormously. Now t[he] of that exegetical work. Weakness, deprivation, loss, exclusion—things the world sees as curses—will, if met with faith in Christ, turn out to be blessings. God's power generally comes to us through our weakness. Ortlund unfolds the implications of this radical, counterintuitive, and countercultural message in ways that are deeply provocative but also profoundly comforting."

Tim Keller, Founding Pastor, Redeemer Presbyterian Church, New York City; Cofounder, Redeemer City to City

"Most Christians think they know the theology of the apostle Paul. But few, I fear, know Paul himself. I have always believed that the best way to discover the heart of this man is by reading and reflecting on 2 Corinthians and the way in which the dawning of the new age transformed this formerly angry Pharisee into the apostle of Jesus Christ. This epistle, to the surprise of many, is my favorite New Testament book. Dane Ortlund's excellent unpacking of its theology only confirms my esteem. If you've never immersed yourself in 2 Corinthians, this short treatment of its primary focus is the place to begin. I trust it will lead you to take a deep dive into the way in which the gospel enabled Paul to find strength in the midst of weakness, peace in the midst of conflict, and hope in the face of constant opposition."

Sam Storms, Founder and President, Enjoying God Ministries

"A theological commentary on this surprisingly neglected New Testament epistle is long overdue. This volume gives us a systematic overview of Christian teaching as found in 2 Corinthians that will be of immense value to students and teachers alike."

Gerald Bray, Research Professor of Divinity, Beeson Divinity School; author, *Biblical Interpretation: Past and Present*

"Dane Ortlund has done us a great service in writing this book: no one should preach through 2 Corinthians without reading it! Writing on 2 Corinthians is often complex and even confused, but this reliable guide is succinct, crystal clear, profound, and, like the letter itself, immeasurably rich. Short enough to serve the preacher well, it manages to handle all the key points of debate deftly. The chapters 'Inaugurated Eschatology' and 'Strength through Weakness' alone are worth the purchase price. I cannot commend this book highly enough."

Gary Millar, Principal, Queensland Theological College; author, *2 Corinthians for You*

Ministry in the New Realm

New Testament Theology

Edited by Thomas R. Schreiner and Brian S. Rosner

Ministry in the New Realm

A Theology of 2 Corinthians

Dane C. Ortlund

WHEATON, ILLINOIS

Series design: Kevin Lipp
First printing 2023
Printed in the United States of America

Trade paperback ISBN: 978-1-4335-7415-3
ePub ISBN: 978-1-4335-7418-4
PDF ISBN: 978-1-4335-7416-0

Library of Congress Cataloging-in-Publication Data

Names: Ortlund, Dane Calvin, author.
Title: Ministry in the new realm : a theology of 2 Corinthians / Dane C. Ortlund.
Description: Wheaton, Illinois : Crossway, 2023. | Series: New Testament theology | Includes bibliographical references and index.
Identifiers: LCCN 2022049378 (print) | LCCN 2022049379 (ebook) | ISBN 9781433574153 (trade paperback) | ISBN 9781433574153 (pdf) | ISBN 9781433574184 (epub)
Subjects: LCSH: Bible. Corinthians, 2nd—Theology.
Classification: LCC BS2675.52 .O78 2023 (print) | LCC BS2675.52 (ebook) | DDC 227/.306—dc23/eng/20230517
LC record available at https://lccn.loc.gov/2022049378
LC ebook record available at https://lccn.loc.gov/2022049379

To Dr. Hans Bayer,
teacher, discipler, encourager, friend

"This quest may be attempted by the weak with as much hope as the strong. Yet such is oft the course of deeds that move the wheels of the world: small hands do them because they must, while the eyes of the great are elsewhere."

ELROND, AT THE COUNCIL OF ELROND,
J. R. R. TOLKIEN, *THE LORD OF THE RINGS*

Contents

Series Preface

THERE ARE REMARKABLY FEW TREATMENTS of the big ideas of single books of the New Testament. Readers can find brief coverage in Bible dictionaries, in some commentaries, and in New Testament theologies, but such books are filled with other information and are not devoted to unpacking the theology of each New Testament book in its own right. Technical works concentrating on various themes of New Testament theology often have a narrow focus, treating some aspect of the teaching of, say, Matthew or Hebrews in isolation from the rest of the book's theology.

The New Testament Theology series seeks to fill this gap by providing students of Scripture with readable book-length treatments of the distinctive teaching of each New Testament book or collection of books. The volumes approach the text from the perspective of biblical theology. They pay due attention to the historical and literary dimensions of the text, but their main focus is on presenting the teaching of particular New Testament books about God and his relations to the world on their own terms, maintaining sight of the Bible's overarching narrative and Christocentric focus. Such biblical theology is of fundamental importance to biblical and expository preaching and informs exegesis, systematic theology, and Christian ethics.

The twenty volumes in the series supply comprehensive, scholarly, and accessible treatments of theological themes from an evangelical perspective. We envision them being of value to students, preachers, and interested laypeople. When preparing an expository sermon series, for example, pastors can find a healthy supply of informative commentaries, but there are few options for coming to terms with the overall teaching of each book of the New Testament. As well as being useful in sermon and Bible study preparation, the volumes will also be of value as textbooks in college and seminary exegesis classes. Our prayer is that they contribute to a deeper understanding of and commitment to the kingdom and glory of God in Christ.

Sometimes regarded as Paul's impassioned, heartfelt, but disjointed response to disparate problems in the church, 2 Corinthians presents distinctive challenges for readers wishing to learn from its teaching on a range of topics. The letter covers everything from the new covenant and the signs of an apostle to reconciliation and generous giving. Dane Ortlund's *Ministry in the New Realm* locates the common thread throughout 2 Corinthians in the inauguration of the kingdom of God, which reveals God's power through human weakness. Read with this framework in mind, Ortlund's volume unpacks the letter's remarkably comprehensive vision for Christlike ministry that is both profoundly theological as well as thoroughly practical.

Thomas R. Schreiner and Brian S. Rosner

Abbreviations

BDAG	Frederick W. Danker, Walter Bauer, William F. Arndt, and F. Wilbur Gingrich. *Greek-English Lexicon of the New Testament and Other Early Christian Literature.* 3rd ed. Chicago: University of Chicago Press, 2000
BNTC	Black's New Testament Commentaries
BTNT	Biblical Theology of the New Testament
CTJ	*Calvin Theological Journal*
ETL	*Ephemerides Theologicae Louvanienses*
HTR	*Harvard Theological Review*
JETS	*Journal of the Evangelical Theological Society*
JSNT	*Journal for the Study of the New Testament*
JTS	*Journal of Theological Studies*
LCL	Loeb Classical Library
LNTS	Library of New Testament Studies
LXX	Septuagint
Neot	*Neotestamentica*
NICNT	New International Commentary on the New Testament
NIGTC	New International Greek Testament Commentary
NSBT	New Studies in Biblical Theology
NTS	*New Testament Studies*
SNTSMS	Society for New Testament Studies Monograph Series
SSBT	Short Studies in Biblical Theology

Them	*Themelios*
TynBul	*Tyndale Bulletin*
WBC	Word Biblical Commentary
WUNT	Wissenschaftliche Untersuchungen zum Neuen Testament

Introduction

A Letter Like No Other

THE OVERARCHING THEOLOGICAL MESSAGE of 2 Corinthians is this: in the new realm that was inaugurated when Jesus ascended and the Spirit descended, life and ministry are flipped upside down such that God's strength interlocks not with human strength and sufficiency but with human weakness and pain.

That summary has two basic parts: (1) we today live in the dawning new realm that the Old Testament anticipated, the new creation that was expected to come at the end of history; and (2) the basic pattern for joy and growth in this new realm is paradoxical, as life comes through death, strength through weakness, comfort through affliction, and so on—as was the pattern of Christ himself. These two points will form the first and last chapters of this book, with the intervening chapters exploring other key themes of 2 Corinthians, all flowing out of the new creational age in which believers find themselves between the first and second comings of Christ. But before we get into the heart of this study and the theology of 2 Corinthians, let's pause to consider this epistle from a broader perspective.

There is nothing in the Bible quite like 2 Corinthians. The present volume explores and synthesizes the theology of this letter. That is appropriate, as the message of the Bible and of each of its sixty-six books is centrally theological—that is, revealing of God and his ways with humanity. The Bible also has rich historical and literary qualities, but these serve the more basic theological message. This is particularly noticeable in the letters of Paul. "The preaching and teaching of Paul," Geerhardus Vos says in his opening sentence of an essay outlining Paul's theology, "possess more than any other New Testament body of truth a theological character."[1]

So we will reflect in this volume on the theology of 2 Corinthians. And in the first sentence of this introduction I have given a summary of what that theology is. But before focusing on this, we should note the distinctiveness of 2 Corinthians from a broader angle. In at least four ways, this letter of Paul's stands apart from the other letters we have in the New Testament: this letter is more autobiographical, more raw, more interpersonal, and more defensive. These four qualities overlap to varying degrees, but they are still worth considering independently, given how distinctive each is throughout 2 Corinthians. These features are not so much the *content* of the letter's theology as much as they are what *shape* its theology, so it is worth beginning our study by getting these elements before us.

Autobiographical

Every reader of Paul's letters faces the unique challenge of hearing only one side of a conversation. Like hearing someone speaking on the phone on the other side of the room, we do not know the exact situation to which the apostles are responding in their letters. It would be easy to make too much of this challenge; God has given us precisely what we need for life and salvation in the sixty-six books of Scripture, including the letters. Yet the challenge, while ordered by God's wisdom, remains.

In 2 Corinthians, however, this difficulty is lessened through the pervasive autobiographical details Paul divulges. Throughout this epistle we hear him explicitly identifying events of his own life and ministry to the church at Corinth. No letter in the New Testament

---

1   Geerhardus Vos, "The Theology of Paul," in *Redemptive History and Biblical Interpretation: The Collected Shorter Writings of Geerhardus Vos*, ed. R. B. Gaffin Jr. (Phillipsburg, NJ: P&R, 1980), 355.

is pure systematic theology, of course. Every letter bears the marks of personal context between apostle and recipient church. And yet opening to 2 Corinthians immediately after a reading of, say, Romans or Ephesians, we are quickly struck by the autobiographical transparency with which Paul writes.

Paul speaks of his near-death experience in Asia (1:8–11), his travel plans (1:15–24; 2:12–13), his interaction with an offending sinner (2:5–11), his friendship with Titus (7:6–7, 13–15), a letter he previously wrote to the Corinthians and the damaging effect it had on their relationship (7:8–9), his fruitful fundraising in Macedonia (8:1–5), and his own sufferings throughout chapters 10–13.

The Bible is not a sort of pure doctrine that has floated down from heaven from the very throne of God, giving us divine truth in the form of timeless abstraction. No, the Bible is mediated to us through fellow fallen human beings, such as the apostle Paul. And the personal circumstances of each biblical author form an evident part of their writing. God speaks to us today through the earthy and painful lives and minds of ordinary men and women. In 2 Corinthians, perhaps more than in any other book of the Bible, we see this.

Raw

It's difficult to know exactly what word to use, but I think you know what I mean by the word *raw*—Paul's emotions are right on the surface of the letter, and he isn't trying to hide them. The letter is pervasively and unashamedly impassioned.

Paul never views his churches as mere converts or numbers. He views them as his sheep, his disciples, his spiritual charge—even his own children. And while it is not clear precisely what all the dysfunctions in the church at Corinth were, it is evident that Paul's concern is not ultimately with his own reputation or with what the Corinthians think of him. He is concerned centrally with the way that a worldly pattern of thinking is infecting the church and eroding their own soul health.

One could hardly blame a young Christian for turning to 2 Corinthians for the first time and thinking: "Am I reading the *Bible* here?" Perhaps in our own early journey with Scripture we had read the soaring creation narrative of Genesis, the thundering Sinai episode as the law is given in Exodus, the dancing poetry of the Psalms, the earthy wisdom of Proverbs, the enrapturing teachings of the Lord Jesus in the Gospels, or the piercing gospel logic of Romans, and then we read Holy Scripture saying:

I call God to witness against me—it was to spare you that I refrained from coming again to Corinth. (2 Cor. 1:23)

I am acting with great boldness toward you; I have great pride in you; I am filled with comfort. (2 Cor. 7:4)

Accept me as a fool, so that I too may boast. (2 Cor. 11:16)

Are they servants of Christ? I am a better one—I am talking like a madman—with far greater labors, far more imprisonments, with countless beatings, and often near death. (2 Cor. 11:23)

Is this really Holy Scripture? Indeed. To be sure, the epistle of 2 Corinthians is unapologetically impassioned—but what else would we expect of a document that is the very word of God? God himself is impassioned. He is not the deity of a Platonic worldview, distant and cold and detached. He is not a calculating chessmaster, moving pieces on the chessboard of the world in a dispassionate way. No, this is the God who speaks of his people as his own bride and of their faithlessness as unspeakable harlotry. This is the God whose heart churns within him as he considers their wickedness:

How can I give you up, O Ephraim?
    How can I hand you over, O Israel?
How can I make you like Admah?
    How can I treat you like Zeboiim?

My heart recoils within me;

my compassion grows warm and tender. (Hos. 11:8)

And ultimately this is the God who rolls up his sleeves and enters into the muck and mess of this desperately fallen world in the incarnation of his own Son.

God is impassible, unable to be pained or swayed by any outside influence, but that is not to say he is not impassioned. So when we come to 2 Corinthians and find the word of this God mediated to us through the raw passion of an anguished apostle, we ought not be overly surprised.

As we explore the theology of 2 Corinthians, then, we should not bracket out or skip over the parts of this letter where Paul is pleading, longing, frustrated, or indignant. All of it is God's word to us, and all of it informs the overall theological message of the book.

Interpersonal

Third, 2 Corinthians is uniquely interpersonal, or relational, in nature. By this I mean that throughout the letter we see Paul referring to his own colleagues and also speaking to the Corinthians about his relationship with them.

Right from the start Paul identifies his letter as coming from him "and Timothy our brother" (1:1). It is not unusual for Paul to pull in a colleague or two as he greets a recipient church. What is unusual is that he would loop back to interpersonal realities so pervasively throughout the letter. Perhaps only Galatians offers a comparable level of interpersonal reflection. In both letters, reflection on the vertical (how God and people relate) is strongly complemented by reflection on the horizontal (how people relate with other people). This dual dynamic is captured representatively in the final few verses of 2 Corinthians:

Finally, brothers, rejoice. Aim for restoration, comfort one another, agree with one another, live in peace; and the God of love and peace will be with you. Greet one another with a holy kiss. All the saints greet you. (13:11–13) (*horizontal*)

The grace of the Lord Jesus Christ and the love of God and the fellowship of the Holy Spirit be with you all. (13:14) (*vertical*)

But it isn't just the opening few verses and the closing few verses that surface Paul's horizontal concerns. Paul spends the bulk of the first two chapters of the letter seeking to salvage his apparently fragile relationship with the Corinthian church, going to some length to justify his change of travel plans that led him to write the Corinthians a letter instead of visiting them in person. As we arrive in 2 Corinthians 7 we once more find ourselves in an extended interpersonal reflection as Paul speaks of the comforting presence of Titus, who reassured Paul and Timothy of the Corinthians' good will.

Chapters 8 and 9 are rightly thought of as having to do with money and financial generosity, but both chapters are filled with interpersonal considerations—the sending of the brother famous for preaching (8:18–19), for example, or the commendation of Titus (8:16–24). As Paul himself says, through these actions Paul and his companions "aim at what is honorable not only in the Lord's sight but also in the sight of man" (8:21)—in other words, not only that which has to do with the vertical but also that which has to do with the horizontal.

And of course chapters 10–13 transition from positive interpersonal realities in Paul's life to negative ones, though the chapters maintain a strong horizontal focus, as Paul castigates the spiritual fraudulence of the "super-apostles" (11:5) and defends his own apostolic credentials. And we also continue to see the depths to which Paul's heart and welfare are lovingly bound up with that of the Corinthians. In 12:21, for example, Paul reflects on his impending visit to Corinth and speaks of *himself* being humbled by God if the *Corinthians* have remained in sin—not how many Christian leaders today view their relationship to their people. In 13:5, similarly, Paul expresses hope that the Corinthians will pass the test of spiritual maturity—but then turns around in 13:6 and says that if the Corinthians fail, it is also Paul's own failure. In texts such as these, unique in the Pauline corpus, the apostle binds his own welfare with that of the Corinthians in a most striking way.

Paul's defense of his ministry in these closing chapters to the epistle leads us into the fourth and final distinctive mark of 2 Corinthians.

Defensive

In no other letter is Paul so manifestly eager for his ministry to be validated.

This may raise questions for some: Is Paul being petty? Is he overly concerned for his good name? Is he violating Proverbs 27:2: "Let another praise you, and not your own mouth"? Is Paul falling prey to the common fallen impulse to self-justify rather than collapsing into the freedom of letting God be the one to defend him?

On the one hand, Paul is, like all of us, a fallen human being. He is not any less in need of God's saving mercy than we are. On the other hand, 2 Corinthians is inspired and inerrant, and we must be careful not to impugn Scripture as tainted in any way that would be out of accord with our conviction about Scripture.

The answer is that apparently there is a third option beyond (1) unhealthy defensiveness and (2) modestly and quietly avoiding any defense of oneself whatsoever. That third option is healthy defending of oneself—a defense that is ruthlessly objective with regard to oneself because the ultimate purpose is not self-concern but concern for something outside of you—for example, the truth of the gospel or (in the case of 2 Corinthians) the nature of truly apostolic ministry in the new age, in which weakness and rejection are legitimate badges of divinely sanctioned authenticity.

If Paul does not defend himself but allows the Corinthians to be beguiled by the super-apostles' fleshly "theology of glory" as opposed to the "theology of the cross" (to use Luther's phrases[2]), then these believers whom he loves will continue their slide into the enticing stupor of a Christianity that is outwardly impressive. The Corinthians' spiritual welfare, not Paul's name, is what drives Paul's defense of his ministry. This is an important model for us in Christian ministry today. While we must be appropriately self-suspicious and vigilant not to seek to justify ourselves before God or men (that is the gospel's job, not ours), it is not only permissible but imperative that we defend ourselves when the attacks on us, if victorious, will result in the spiritual impoverishing of those under our care.

Summarizing the Theology of 2 Corinthians

These, then, are some of the distinctive elements of 2 Corinthians—not the theology itself but features that shape the way the theology of this book comes to us. Let us now briefly consider the theology of this book, then, mindful of the above characteristics of the letter. The rest of the chapters of this book will explore the various prominent theological themes that make up this summary.

Above I identified the theology of 2 Corinthians:

> In the new realm that was inaugurated when Jesus ascended and the Spirit descended, life and ministry are flipped upside down such that God's strength interlocks not with human strength and sufficiency but with human weakness and pain.

The two primary emphases are inaugurated eschatology and strength through weakness. Inaugurated eschatology is, we could say, the stage on which 2 Corinthians is played out, and strength through weakness the costume. The former (inaugurated eschatology) is the broader context or framing, and the latter (strength through weakness) the

---

2 See especially Luther's "Heidelberg Disputation (1518)," in *Martin Luther's Basic Theological Writings*, ed. Timothy F. Lull and William R. Russell, 3rd ed. (Minneapolis: Fortress, 2012), 14–25.

specific individual and existential experience of those who belong to that broader context.

But beyond these two macro-themes to 2 Corinthians are other vital building blocks, without which these two themes disintegrate. Some of these are explicit in the above theological summary (Jesus, the Spirit, pain), while others are more implicit but remain important themes for 2 Corinthians as a whole (Satan, friendship, heaven). And all these together make up the chapters of the present study.

Throughout this project, I am seeking to be ruthlessly focused on 2 Corinthians itself, letting it stand forth in all its distinctiveness. Themes that are important to Paul's theology broadly understood but minimally on display in 2 Corinthians will be accordingly treated lightly or not at all. For example, right at the heart of Paul's theology, taking Acts and his thirteen epistles all into view with a wide-angle lens, is the notion of grace, rightly put front and center in John Barclay's groundbreaking 2015 monograph,[3] as well as in other studies.[4] Yet grace as "incongruous" gift (to use Barclay's adjective) is virtually nowhere in sight in 2 Corinthians—at least as it is popularly understood, as God's gratuitous goodness to people. Paul certainly uses the word *charis*, the standard Pauline term for "grace," but in this letter it normally denotes some kind of gracious human activity (horizontally), not divine gift (vertically).[5] Thus Frank Thielman's proposal of the "center" of Paul's theology as "God's graciousness toward his weak and sinful creatures,"[6] while about as good as any, does not sit particularly comfortably with 2 Corinthians. I take Richard Gaffin's proposal for a center to Paul's theology as more broadly encompassing of the particular message of 2 Corinthians: "The

---

3   John M. G. Barclay, *Paul and the Gift* (Grand Rapids, MI: Eerdmans, 2015).

4   E.g., Jonathan A. Linebaugh, *The Word of the Cross: Reading Paul* (Grand Rapids, MI: Eerdmans, 2022), though the focus throughout is more narrowly Romans and Galatians. Moo begins his synthesizing discussion of Paul's theology with an exploration of "grace." Douglas J. Moo, *A Theology of Paul and His Letters: The Gift of the New Realm in Christ*, BTNT (Grand Rapids, MI: Zondervan Academic, 2021), 377–78.

5   E.g., 2 Cor. 1:15; 8:4, 6, 7, 19.

6   Frank Thielman, *Theology of the New Testament: A Canonical and Synthetic Approach* (Grand Rapids, MI: Zondervan, 2005), 232.

center of his theology is the death and resurrection of Christ in their eschatological significance."[7]

A second example of an otherwise major Pauline concept that does not figure prominently in 2 Corinthians is the notorious matter of the "law" in Paul and how he understands the Mosaic code to function in the life of the believer in the new covenant era. While any treatment of Paul's theology as a whole must grapple with Paul and the law (the two editors of the present series having provided two of the best[8]), not a single instance of *nomos* occurs in 2 Corinthians. Paul does reflect at length on the distinctive differences between the old covenant and the new covenant in 2 Corinthians 3, but even there the focus is not on the "law" specifically (i.e., Mosaic code) but rather the passing glory of the old realm and the inaugurated glory of the new realm. Questions of the ongoing relevance of the Mosaic code for today's Christians, then, while pressing in terms of Pauline theology generally, do not naturally present themselves from a study of 2 Corinthians specifically.

These two otherwise central Pauline themes of "grace" and "law" are but two examples of the way we must allow 2 Corinthians to speak on its own terms and not read broader Pauline concerns into it, if we are to let the distinctive contribution of this unique epistle shine forth clearly.

If otherwise vital Pauline notions such as "grace" and "law" are nowhere near the heart of Paul's concerns in 2 Corinthians, what is the heart or center or core burden of this letter? There is more than one equally valid perspective on this, so we should avoid any forced or narrowly dogmatic answer to this question. But we must right away note the pervasive presence in 2 Corinthians of notions associated with the dawning of the latter-day eschaton. One way to make this point is in Douglas Moo's comprehensive treatment of Paul's theology. He identifies "five basic 'umbrella' blessings"[9] of this new aeon: new cove-

---

7   Richard B. Gaffin Jr., *By Faith, Not by Sight: Paul and the Order of Salvation*, 2nd ed. (Phillipsburg, NJ: P&R, 2013), 29.

8   Thomas R. Schreiner, *The Law and Its Fulfillment: A Pauline Theology of Law* (Grand Rapids, MI: Baker, 1998); Brian Rosner, *Paul and the Law: Keeping the Commandments of God*, NSBT 31 (Downers Grove, IL: IVP Academic, 2013).

9   Moo, *Theology of Paul*, 464.

nant, the Spirit, new creation, salvation, and life.[10] Strikingly, as we will see in the pages of this study, *all five* are conspicuously present in 2 Corinthians. Indeed, 2 Corinthians is probably the best option for the Pauline letter that most robustly brings together these five new realm blessings most consistently.

With the inaugurated new realm as the controlling context of 2 Corinthians, I will retain this context in mind as I proceed through each chapter, unfolding the primary theological topics of this letter as follows:

1. Inaugurated Eschatology: The Framework for New Realm Ministry
2. Jesus Christ: The Launcher of New Realm Ministry
3. The Spirit: The Sign of New Realm Ministry
4. Satan: The Enemy of New Realm Ministry
5. Friendship: The Method of New Realm Ministry
6. Heaven: The Hope of New Realm Ministry
7. Strength through Weakness: The Secret to New Realm Ministry

We begin, then, by setting out in more detail the framing of the whole letter: inaugurated eschatology.

---

10 Moo, *Theology of Paul*, 464–69.

1

Inaugurated Eschatology

The Framework for New Realm Ministry

Inaugurated Eschatology in the New Testament Generally

The central message of the New Testament is soteriological—a message of saving grace in Jesus Christ for undeserving sinners, both Jew and Gentile. But this salvation does not appear in a historical vacuum. The coming of Jesus and the salvation he brings is a point of historical culmination; he arrived "when the fullness of time had come" (Gal. 4:4). But this historical culminating point in Jesus is not simply a particularly decisive event in history. It is a new beginning.[1] Specifically, it is the

---

1   Ridderbos: "What is meant by this 'fullness of the time' is not only the maturation of a specific matter in the great framework of redemptive history, but the fulfillment of the time in an absolute sense. The time of the world has come to a conclusion with Christ's advent. However much this fulfillment still bears a provisional character and the perfectum is followed yet again by a *futurum*, nevertheless the pleroma of the time or of the times is here spoken of as a matter that has already taken effect and thus in principle has been settled." Herman Ridderbos, *Paul: An Outline of His Theology*, trans. John Richard de Witt (Grand Rapids, MI: Eerdmans, 1975), 44–45. Ridderbos is speaking here of Gal. 4:4 specifically and beginning his treatment of the basic structures of Paul's theology more generally. Vos similarly comments that the phrase "the fullness of time" in Gal. 4:4 "certainly means more than that the time was ripe for the introduction of Christ into the world: the fullness of the time means the end of that aeon and the commencement of another world-period." Geerhardus Vos, "The Eschatological Aspect of the Pauline Conception of the Spirit," in *Redemptive History and Biblical Interpretation: The Collected Shorter Writings of Geerhardus Vos*, ed. R. B. Gaffin Jr. (Phillipsburg, NJ: P&R, 1980), 93.

beginning of the new creational age that the Old Testament longed for.[2] Two thousand years ago the latter days dawned. The eschaton (lit. "last time") arrived. It has yet to be completed—a point that must not be lost sight of (and which is clear in 2 Corinthians, such as when Paul anticipates the future "day of our Lord Jesus" in 1:14). But the present evangelical consciousness tends to focus on what we await, not what we already have, so in the present study I am going to push hard in the direction of what we already have. And so I say with force and clarity that while the central message of the New Testament is soteriological, the overarching context of that salvation is *eschatological*. Running just under the surface throughout 2 Corinthians and the entire New Testament and surfacing at times explicitly is the framework of inaugurated eschatology from which all of Paul's thinking and writing flow.

It is worth clarifying exactly what we're talking about from the perspective of the New Testament as a whole before going specifically to 2 Corinthians. Some contemporary New Testament scholars have held inaugurated eschatology front and center in their theologies of the New Testament—G. K. Beale (influenced by Geerhardus Vos), for example, and Thomas Schreiner (influenced by George Ladd).[3] But I am not aware of any treatment of 2 Corinthians in a focused way that self-consciously maintains the lens of inaugurated eschatology.

In a standard systematic theology text, "eschatology" refers to matters pertaining purely to the future and comprises the last chapter of the book. "Eschatology" as I will be using it in this book refers not to the future but to the future-as-having-been-launched-back-into-the-present. And so we call it inaugurated eschatology—the last things have been inaugurated, decisively begun, already.[4] What was expected

---

2   An artful and brief exposition of the biblical narrative as one of creation to new creation can be found in Frank Thielman, *The New Creation and the Storyline of Scripture*, SSBT (Wheaton, IL: Crossway, 2021).

3   G. K. Beale, *New Testament Biblical Theology: The Unfolding of the Old Testament in the New* (Grand Rapids, MI: Baker Academic, 2011); Thomas R. Schreiner, *New Testament Theology: Magnifying God in Christ* (Grand Rapids, MI: Baker Academic, 2008).

4   It is a bit ironic that the past century's main pioneer of this point places "eschatology" last in his magnum opus. See Geerhardus Vos, *Reformed Dogmatics*, ed. and trans. R. B. Gaffin Jr. (Bellingham, WA: Lexham, 2020).

THE FRAMEWORK FOR NEW REALM MINISTRY   15

to happen at the end of history has been launched back and dropped into the middle of history.[5] Christ's first coming—especially his resurrection—began the eschaton, and his second coming will escalate the eschaton into its full blossoming. William Manson expressed this vividly in 1953:

> When we turn to the New Testament, we pass from the climate of prediction to that of fulfillment. The things which God had foreshadowed by the lips of His holy prophets He has now, in part at least, brought to accomplishment. . . . The supreme sign of the Eschaton is the resurrection of Jesus and the descent of the Holy Spirit on the Church. The resurrection of Jesus is not simply a sign which God has granted in favor of His Son, but is the inauguration, the entrance into history, of the times of the End. Christians, therefore, have entered through the Christ into the new age. . . . What had been predicted in Holy Scripture as to happen to Israel or to man in the Eschaton has happened to and in Jesus.[6]

The reason that it often does not feel as if the eschaton has in fact arrived is that the old age, the realm of sin and death, continued existing alongside the new realm that dawned in Christ. When Christ returns, that old realm will once and for all cease. We can see why theologians speak, then, of "the overlap of the ages." We who live between Christ's two comings live in a strange tension, one that was not experienced by Old Testament saints (for whom there was old realm but not new realm) nor will be experienced by citizens of the new earth (for whom there will be new realm but not

---

5 I have been influenced by the strong emphasis Oscar Cullmann places on the coming of Christ as taking place at "the midpoint" of history, though Cullmann is perhaps less clear on all that has been inaugurally fulfilled at that midpoint; see Oscar Cullmann, *Christ and Time: The Primitive Christian Conception of Time and History*, trans. F. V. Filson (London: SCM, 1962); Oscar Cullmann, *Salvation in History* (New York: Harper and Row, 1967).

6 William Manson, "Eschatology and the New Testament," in *Scottish Journal of Theology, Occasional Papers* 2 (Edinburgh: Oliver & Boyd, 1953), 6.

old realm). We must immediately clarify that this does not mean believers are "split down the middle," half of each believer belonging to the old realm and half to the new realm. Many days it may feel that way—or indeed, that we belong far more to the old realm than the new! But the clear and persistent teaching of the New Testament is that our basic identity is as citizens of the new creational age that dawned when Christ was raised from the dead. Our spiritual ID card now says "new realm" where it used to say "old realm." "Our citizenship is in heaven" (Phil. 3:20).

A word on terminology: I will be using the word *realm* in this book in an effort to communicate as clearly as I can, though this is not the only serviceable word. Other ways we could describe this new period of history are new creation, new era, new order, new covenant, new aeon, new world, new epoch, new kingdom, new age, and so on.[7] I prefer *new realm* as that which is, in my judgment, least open to misunderstanding. It also usefully overlaps semantically with the language of "kingdom" in Jesus's teaching in the Synoptic Gospels. Douglas Moo uses this verbiage in his 2021 treatment of Paul's theology, and I found it useful there, so I gratefully carry forward that language here.[8]

Let's press more deeply now into what I mean by inaugurated eschatology or the dawning of the new realm. When we speak of the new realm having erupted in the middle of history, what are the actual biblical markers sustaining such a claim?

---

7   Throughout this volume I will use several of these monikers synonymously with "new realm," and in particular "new creation" and "new creational realm" as analogous titles to "new realm." But for the sake of consistency, I will most often use "realm" language. For a specific defense of new creation as the key unifying center of New Testament theology, see G. K. Beale, "The Eschatological Conception of New Testament Theology," in *"The Reader Must Understand": Eschatology in Bible and Theology*, ed. K. E. Brower and M. W. Elliott (Downers Grove, IL: InterVarsity Press, 1997), 11–52.

8   Douglas J. Moo, *A Theology of Paul and His Letters: The Gift of the New Realm in Christ*, BTNT (Grand Rapids, MI: Zondervan Academic, 2021). Moo himself is clear on the centrality of inaugurated eschatology in the New Testament—e.g., "The dominant and distinctive feature of all New Testament teaching is the way the early believers celebrate their identity as members of the new realm" (374).

We can look at it this way: What were the major events or markers that God's people in the Old Testament were anticipating? What, according to the prophetic ministry they had received, were they expecting to happen at the end of history? When Mark tells us that Joseph of Arimathea "was also himself looking for the kingdom of God" (Mark 15:43), what exactly was the content of that eager expectation?

From the perspective of the Old Testament, a constellation of world-shaking events would signal and usher in the latter days and the new creational kingdom, or what we're calling "the new realm":[9]

1. Messiah would come.
2. God's enemies would be defeated.
3. The fall in Eden would be undone.
4. Sin would be judged.
5. The nations would stream to Jerusalem.
6. God's people would be vindicated over their enemies.
7. God's latter-day kingdom would be ushered in.
8. The dead would be raised.

Here's the key point: from the vantage point of the New Testament, *every one of these expectations has been fulfilled*:

1. Messiah has come (Rom. 1:3–4).
2. God's enemies were decisively triumphed over—not on a battle-field but on a cross (Col. 2:13–15).
3. A second Adam has succeeded where the first Adam failed—in being tempted by Satan, for example (Luke 3:38–4:13). More-over, the second Adam's exorcisms (driving demons out of people) were a middle-of-time accomplishing of what Adam failed to do (driving Satan out of Eden).

9 The content of these next few paragraphs has been adapted from Dane Ortlund, "Bible Q&A: Why Are There Two Testaments in the Bible?," Crossway, March 4, 2014, https://www.crossway.org/. Used by permission.

4. Sin was judged once and for all at the cross. The cross was the end-time judgment on sin, all funneled down onto one man (Rom. 5:9; 1 Thess. 5:9).
5. The Gentiles are now flooding into the kingdom as never before (Rom. 15:8–27).
6. God's people have been vindicated in their justification (Rom. 5:1). The declaration of "innocent" anticipated at the end of time has been announced in the present based on a middle-of-history event.
7. As Jesus himself announced, the kingdom is here (Mark 1:15; cf. Acts 20:25; 28:31; Rom. 14:17). We are now in the latter-day kingdom or realm (Heb. 1:2).
8. In Christ, the dead have been raised (Eph. 2:6; Col. 3:1; cf. Rom. 6:4).

The message of the New Testament is not that some of the Old Testament anticipations have been fulfilled and some haven't. The message of the New Testament is that *all* of the Old Testament anticipations have been fulfilled—but in an already / not yet way. A future consummation is still needed at every point. We call it *inaugurated* eschatology, not *fulfilled* eschatology. But the decisive moment has nevertheless already quietly taken place in the person and work of Jesus.

The preceding analysis does not mean that the Old Testament saints or prophets were wrong in expecting all eight of the above promises to occur at the end of human history. They saw truly, but they saw from a distance. Geerhardus Vos uses the image of mountain peaks, helpfully communicating that while from a distance the peaks may look next to one another, one may actually discover a great distance between various mountain peaks once one arrives in the mountains themselves.[10]

The Significance of Resurrection for Inaugurated Eschatology

That eighth and last point above, about the dead being raised, is particularly significant and requires a bit of further reflection. In speaking of the launching of the eschaton, we must zero in on the resurrection

---

10 Vos, *Reformed Dogmatics*, 1095–96.

as the key event that launched the new realm. That event should not be viewed in isolation from the entire "Christ event" (as some theologians refer to it)—his virgin birth, sinless life, and atoning death (leading up to his resurrection); and his bodily ascension, present intercession, and impending return (flowing out from his resurrection). But the New Testament does appear to present his rising as the decisive moment in causing the eschatological sun to rise on the world stage.

This is evident, for example, in the repeated centralizing of Christ's resurrection in the apostles' preaching in Acts. And toward the end of Paul's other letter to the church at Corinth, we have the New Testament's clearest teaching on the eschatological import of Christ's resurrection. There Paul writes,

> But in fact Christ has been raised from the dead, the firstfruits of those who have fallen asleep. For as by a man came death, by a man has come also the resurrection of the dead. For as in Adam all die, so also in Christ shall all be made alive. But each in his own order: Christ the firstfruits, then at his coming those who belong to Christ. (1 Cor. 15:20–23)

In using the Old Testament agricultural image of the "firstfruits" (*aparchē*), Paul is doing two important things. First, he is vitally and organically linking together Christ's resurrection with ours. Throughout 1 Corinthians 15, Paul argues both ways—not only saying that without Christ's resurrection, believers will have no resurrection, but also arguing that without our resurrection, not even Christ has been raised (1 Cor. 15:12–20). Second, he is saying that the final resurrection that was expected to happen to all the saints at the end of the age *has, in Christ's raising, already begun.* The wondrous significance of using the image of "firstfruits" is that the firstfruits is the initial ingathering of one single and whole harvest. The initial gathering guarantees and anticipates the full harvest in due time.[11]

---

11 Paul uses the word *aparchē* a few other times elsewhere in his letters, where it does not have the charged eschatological meaning that it does in 1 Cor. 15:20, 23 but nevertheless helpfully reinforces the notion that an *aparchē* is always the initial ingathering of an

When Jesus was raised from the dead, the new realm began. Eden 2.0 quietly erupted in the middle of history rather than at history's end. He was not raised in the way Lazarus was (John 11:1–44) or the little girl (Mark 5:35–43), both of whom were raised to mortal existence, only to die again.[12] Jesus's resurrection was to an immortal existence, the life of the age to come, which was not pure continuity with one's previous mortal existence (as with, say, Lazarus) but apparently also included discontinuity. I deduce this from the fact that others had difficulty recognizing him (Luke 24:16) and he appeared to be able to defy the laws of physics with regard to a locked door (John 20:19). At the same time, the risen Jesus ate breakfast (John 21:9–13) and let Thomas touch his physical wounds (John 20:27), so apparently the risen life is just as physical as this mortal existence is.

And the teaching of the New Testament is that *believers' resurrection is not only a matter of the future.* It is not as if Jesus's inaugural resurrection merely guarantees ours, though it does do that. During the course of this new realm in between his two comings, any time that a sinner is enabled by the Spirit to exercise faith in Jesus for salvation, that person is immediately and irreversibly united to Christ, and one aspect of what happens is this: that believer experiences resurrection. Not physically but spiritually—and, we should add, literally. To be sure, we must be careful to avoid the overrealized error of Hymeneaus and Philetus, who wrongly taught that "the resurrection has already happened" (2 Tim. 2:18), referring to the final bodily raising of believers. In 2 Corinthians we will see that Paul can speak of a final consummating resurrection yet to come (2 Cor. 4:14). But we must nevertheless press home the point that the key reality in final resurrection has, even now, already taken place. It is not a mere metaphorical resurrection, as if "resurrection" is simply a particularly beautiful way of expressing the wonder of salvation. No, believers are actually raised. The hardest part has been done. The most decisive thing has been accomplished, for they

---

organically connected single harvest (Rom. 11:16; 16:5; 1 Cor. 16:15; and the only other New Testament use, Rev. 14:4).

12 Vos, *Reformed Dogmatics*, 1114.

are joined to a risen Christ. We "have been raised with Christ" (Col. 3:1); Christ was raised, but for us who are in him, God also "raised us up with him" (Eph. 2:6). We are co-resurrected with Jesus. While we await the final consummating reality of that resurrection—the physical component—we are already, in principle and in an inaugurally guaranteeing way, literally-spiritually raised.

Every Aspect of Pauline Theology Is Eschatological

Let us pause and reflect on all we have considered thus far in this chapter. What we are seeing is that rather than eschatology being a final, freestanding element of New Testament theology, *every aspect of New Testament theology is inherently eschatological.* As Vos pithily put it, "to unfold the Apostle's eschatology means to set forth his theology as a whole."[13]

Justification is an eschatological reality because we are once-and-for-all acquitted now, in Christ, but the public vindicating manifestation of that awaits Christ's return. Sanctification is an eschatological reality because in Christ we have been once-and-for-all cleansed positionally, but we await final actual moral cleansing upon Christ's return.[14] Christian living and killing sin is to be understood eschatologically: in Christ, we have become participants in the dawning new creation, and this is our basic identity, so we are empowered and motivated to live in accord with who we most deeply now are. And so on. Beale explains:

> [T]he apostles understood that they were already living in the end-times and that they were to understand their present salvation in Christ to be already an end-time reality. *Every aspect of their salvation was to be conceived of as eschatological in nature.* To put this another way, every major doctrine of the Christian faith has an end-time tint.[15]

13 Geerhardus Vos, *The Pauline Eschatology* (Princeton: Princeton University Press, 1930; repr., Phillipsburg, NJ: P&R, 1994), 11.
14 I am speaking of positional sanctification, not progressive sanctification.
15 Beale, "Eschatological Conception," 18 (emphasis in original).

Even the gospel itself is eschatological. Consider a text such as Mark 1:14–15, the thesis statement of the entire Gospel of Mark: "Jesus came into Galilee, proclaiming the gospel of God, and saying, 'The time is fulfilled, and the kingdom of God is at hand; repent and believe in the gospel.'" Note that Jesus himself presents the gospel as answering a "when" question: "the *time* is fulfilled." The gospel not only answers a "what question" (our sins being forgiven) but also locates us in a certain historical aeon.

It is, therefore, imperative that if we are to understand the theology of 2 Corinthians, we understand it within this broader framework of inaugurated eschatology. This is true for all twenty-seven books of our New Testament, but in the course of this volume we will increasingly see that inaugurated eschatology is not an occasional matter Paul loops into his argument in 2 Corinthians. Rather, an eschatological outlook is always present throughout the letter, sometimes explicit but apparently always implicit. The ceiling lowers on a reader's understanding of the macro coherence and the inner logic of the letter without wearing the "tinted sunglasses" of inaugurated eschatology.

Having clarified generally what I mean by "inaugurated eschatology" throughout this book, we turn now to consider the letter of 2 Corinthians specifically.[16]

Inaugurated Eschatology in 2 Corinthians

In no other chapter of this book will we take so much time before getting to the actual content of 2 Corinthians. But it was necessary to do so in this opening chapter as clarity about the dawning new realm informs all that follows in a paradigmatic way.

It would be inaccurate to suggest that the new realm is the main point of 2 Corinthians. The main point or purpose of 2 Corinthians

---

16 For an extended defense of the eschatological structure of the New Testament as I understand it, see Richard B. Gaffin Jr., *In the Fullness of Time: An Introduction to the Biblical Theology of Acts and Paul* (Wheaton, IL: Crossway, 2022), 245–320. For a verse-by-verse treatment of 2 Corinthians with inaugurated eschatology integrated as a consistent hermeneutical axiom, see Dane Ortlund, *2 Corinthians*, in *Romans–Galatians*, vol. 10 of *ESV Expository Commentary* (Wheaton, IL: Crossway, 2020).

is to spare the Corinthian church from being led astray from gospel health by the super-apostles. But the new realm that Christ inaugurated is indeed the context, without which we will misunderstand text after text in the letter.

Think of a Christian father trying to help his son understand the importance of respecting his teachers at school. The presenting issue is respect for authority, just as the presenting issue for Paul is the peril of the worldly thinking of the super-apostles. But the broader context for the father's instruction, which will always be present and which he will at times appeal to explicitly, is the reality that his son is a part of his family, under his paternal care and love, and belongs not to the world but to his Christian family. Knowing this context provides empowerment and motivation for his son. Similarly, the controlling and all-informing context for 2 Corinthians and the takedown of the super-apostles is the reality that the Corinthian believers are part of the dawning new realm, citizens of the inaugurated kingdom. This is who they now are, and this citizenship provides the wonder, calm, and gratitude that will fortify them to fend off the allure of the super-apostles' impressive veneer.

In the remainder of this chapter we will survey the most conspicuous examples of inaugurated eschatology in 2 Corinthians. These are the places where Paul's pervasive subterranean hermeneutic bubbles to the surface—particularly clear examples, in other words, of how Paul is thinking of human history at every point in his writing. We will pass over the two references to the Spirit as the "guarantee" or "down payment" (2 Cor. 1:22; 5:5), which are among the most notable instances of the beginning of the new realm, because I will handle these below in chapter 3 on the Spirit.

New Covenant, New Creation

We begin with the recognition that in no other letter does Paul explicitly bring together the themes of "new covenant" (2 Cor. 3:6) and "new creation" (5:17) each of which tingles with eschatological significance.

Both phrases are rare in Paul—the *phrases* are rare, not the concept. Here we should remember James Barr's seminal and salutary clarification that words and concepts ought not be held too rigidly apart: a concept may be present where a word is lacking (and contrariwise we must avoid illegitimate totality transfer, importing more into a single word than context warrants).[17] More recently, N. T. Wright has argued for the pervasive presence of the notion of "covenant" in the Old Testament even though the word is relatively infrequent, and Beale has made a similar argument with regard to "creation" in the New Testament.[18] And so we hold open the possibility that the concepts of new covenant and new creation are latent throughout Paul's writings. Indeed, if this book were a survey of all of Paul's writings, I would argue that they are. But as we are focusing only on 2 Corinthians, let us note with interest that only in this letter does he explicitly mention both.

The phrase *kainē diathēkē* ("new covenant") occurs in only one other place in Paul: 1 Corinthians 11:25, which is picking up the words of Jesus in Luke 22:20 in the context of the institution of the Lord's Supper.[19] The phrase *kainē ktisis* ("new creation") also occurs just one other place in Paul: Galatians 6:15, where it is set as the transcending alternative to viewing either circumcision or uncircumcision as informing one's spiritual identity. Both phrases are fraught with eschatological import. The first, "new covenant," reaches all the way back to Exodus and Sinai and signals the fulfillment of the prophecy of Jeremiah 31:31–34 and the whole swath of biblical anticipation that text represents (of a new law giving that is internalized and of forgiveness of sins). The second, "new creation," reaches even further back, to Genesis 1 and the first creation, and picks up the theme of de-creation/re-creation that rumbles through the Old Testament, bringing this hope of a restored

---

17 James Barr, *The Semantics of Biblical Language* (Oxford: Oxford University Press, 1961). An example of a study that examines Paul's understanding of new creation with treatment of 2 Cor. 5:17 but also by recourse to other conceptually overlapping texts (such as Rom. 6:1–11; 7:1–6; Gal. 2:19–20) is Moyer V. Hubbard, *New Creation in Paul's Letters and Thought*, SNTSMS 119 (Cambridge: Cambridge University Press, 2002).

18 N. T. Wright, *The New Testament and the People of God*, vol. 1 of Christian Origins and the Question of God (London: SPCK, 1992), 260, appealing to the same point made by E. P. Sanders, *Paul and Palestinian Judaism: A Comparison of Patterns of Religion* (London: SCM, 1977), 420–29; Beale, "Eschatological Conception," 23–24.

19 This Greek phrase also occurs in Heb. 8:8; 9:15.

Eden to decisive fulfillment. That which is eschatological in Paul is also protological because the coming eschaton would be a new creation—that is, a return to Eden but in an escalated and invincibilized way. Put more simply, the theme of "new creation" signals that eschatology not only looks to the future but also looks to the past. As the Dutch Reformed tradition has helpfully emphasized, God's work of salvation in the New Testament is not sweeping away all that has happened and starting over from scratch but is rather a work of restoration.[20]

The significance of these two texts does not, however, lie only in the two verses in which they occur (2 Cor. 3:6; 5:17). Their significance lies in the context in which each occurs. Second Corinthians 3 and 5—the new covenant chapter and the new creation chapter, respectively—are each extended reflections on the new realm that has dawned in Christ and on what this new realm means for Paul's apostolic ministry vis-à-vis the super-apostles.

To take just the first six verses of 2 Corinthians 3, Paul is defending his apostolic ministry. He uses two arguments to make the broader point that he is truly "commissioned by God" (2:17). In 3:1–3 he argues that the Corinthians themselves and the new life they are experiencing in Christ are the "letter of recommendation" validating Paul's ministry. In making this point Paul alludes to Ezekiel 36 and the promise of the internalization by the Spirit of divine law on the "tablets" of human hearts rather than stone. This is itself a reflection of Paul's conviction about inaugurated eschatology as he is communicating the fulfillment of the prophetic hope in Ezekiel 36 for this kind of radical internalization of God's law and the gift of the Spirit that the Old Testament anticipates at history's end.

In 3:3–6 Paul moves from the Corinthians themselves as validating to Paul's ministry to God as validating his ministry. Paul's legitimacy as an apostle is not based on his own self-resourced credentials. Rather, "our

---

20 A particular focus in the work of Herman Bavinck, as shown in Jan Veenhof, *Nature and Grace in Herman Bavinck*, trans. A. M. Wolters (Sioux Center, IA: Dordt College Press, 2006); Herman Bavinck, *Holy Spirit, Church, and New Creation*, vol. 4 of *Reformed Dogmatics*, ed. J. Bolt, trans. J. Vriend (Grand Rapids, MI: Baker Academic, 2008), 589–730, esp. 715–30.

sufficiency is from God" (2 Cor. 3:5)—but notice how Paul then goes on to explain this divinely resourced sufficiency—"who has made us sufficient to be ministers of a new covenant, not of the letter but of the Spirit. For the letter kills, but the Spirit gives life" (2 Cor. 3:6). Having just alluded to Ezekiel 36, Paul now alludes to Jeremiah 31, which, like Ezekiel 36, emphasizes the future internalizing of God's law in the latter days.

In 2 Corinthians 3:1–6, then, the presenting issue is Paul's rejection of the notion that he is incompetent to serve as a representative of God. But the way in which he argues this is by appealing to the eschaton as having arrived. The new covenant, the final and climactic binding agreement between God and his people that would transcend all previous covenants and ensure his people's spiritual safety, is here. He argues the *what* from the *when*. Paul does not argue for inaugurated eschatology; he argues from it.

This brings us to 2 Corinthians 5, where we find Paul once again assuming that the new realm has dawned and arguing from that reality as he continues to defend his ministry. The literary high point of the second half of the chapter is 5:17: "Therefore, if anyone is in Christ, he is a new creation. The old has passed away; behold, the new has come." As with Romans 8:1, Paul (perhaps in a flurry of apostolic enthusiasm) does not use a verb in the first half of this verse but simply blurts out (rendering the text with wooden literalism): "If anyone in Christ—new creation." The terseness of the syntax suggests that Paul is eager simply to place union with Christ immediately in the broader context of the new creational age that was promised in the Old Testament. Paul is not speaking of union with Christ making one a "new creature," true as that may be conceptually in light of other biblical texts. The point is rather that those in union with Jesus are swept up into the new spiritual cosmos that now exists in between Christ's two advents.

The second half of the verse then drives home the comprehensiveness of this new state of affairs, repeating the language of "new" (*kainos*): "the old things have passed away, behold the new things have come" (my translation). Those united to Christ do not experience a new reality here, a new reality there. Rather, we have been ushered into a completely new sphere of existence. Nor does Paul say, "If anyone is in Christ, he is promised that one day he will be part of the new creation; the old will pass away, the new will come." No, while there remains a vital aspect still to come, Paul's point in 5:17 is the totality of newness that has *now* washed over the believer. This truth anchors the entire second half of 2 Corinthians 5 as Paul explains why it is imperative for the good news to be shared with unbelievers. This reconciliation with God is not merely about a new state of affairs for an individual (though it *is* gloriously that). We become members of the dawning new creational realm. As Vos puts it, reflecting on 2 Corinthians 5:17: "The καινὴ κτίσις spoken of in II Corinthians 5:17 means the beginning of that world-renewal in which all eschatology culminates."[21] And Paul is talking about this being a present reality for those in Christ.

Beyond the broader contexts of 3:1–6 and 5:1–21, we will now consider a handful of other key texts in 2 Corinthians in which the inaugurated eschatology latent throughout this epistle surfaces.

From Glory to Glory (3:18 in the Context of 3:7–18)

Above we briefly considered 2 Corinthians 3:1–6 and its reference to the new covenant. That text goes on in 3:7–18 to draw out a sustained comparison and contrast between two realms: the old realm (of the law, condemnation, death, and lesser glory) and the new realm (of the Spirit, righteousness, life, and greater glory). Paul reflects on the veil that Moses would wear in Exodus so that his radiant face would not overwhelm the Israelites, and he makes an analogy with new covenant believers, saying that in the dawning eschaton, turning to Christ takes away the spiritual veil that lies over our hearts. Paul makes clear that the new realm glory brought by Christ is "permanent" (3:11) as opposed to the passing glory of the old realm; this is why I speak throughout this study of the new realm as having been "launched" or "inaugurated"—it has begun, never to pass away. The climax of the passage is 3:18: "And we all, with unveiled face, beholding the glory of the Lord,

---

21 Vos, "The Eschatological Aspect," 93–94. Similarly Gaffin, *In the Fullness of Time*, 255–61.

are being transformed into the same image from one degree of glory to another. For this comes from the Lord who is the Spirit."

Most English translations understand the phrase *apo doxēs eis doxan* (lit. "from glory to glory") as the ESV does: "from one degree of glory to another." The reader of the English text is thus confined to understand the text as denoting individual gradual spiritual experience. It is possible that this is what the text means. But I think it more likely, given the broader context of 2 Corinthians 3, that Paul has in mind two aeons of glory, two epochs—two *realms*, as I have been calling them. Paul has just been exploring a sustained contrast between two different eras of redemptive history, and the most heavily repeated attribution of each one is its relative glory. It is worth getting the key verses out in front of us:

> Now if the ministry of death, carved in letters on stone, came with such glory that the Israelites could not gaze at Moses' face because of its glory, which was being brought to an end, will not the ministry of the Spirit have even more glory? For if there was glory in the ministry of condemnation, the ministry of righteousness must far exceed it in glory. Indeed, in this case, what once had glory has come to have no glory at all, because of the glory that surpasses it. For if what was being brought to an end came with glory, much more will what is permanent have glory. (2 Cor. 3:7–11)

I have underlined the references to *doxa* to highlight this primary focus here. If Paul has been contrasting two different realms throughout 2 Corinthians 3, and has been doing so in terms of glory, then when we hear him refer to glory in 3:18 we should be encouraged to understand it in an aeonic way likewise. As we behold the glory of Christ, we are transformed from the glory of the old realm into the glory of the new realm.[22]

---

22 I have made an extended exegetical defense of this reading in Dane C. Ortlund, "'From Glory to Glory': 2 Corinthians 3:18 in Biblical-Theological Perspective," *CTJ* 54, no. 1 (2019): 11–33.

Light Shining in Darkness (4:6 in the Context of 4:1–6)

Paul continues the language of veiling and glory in 2 Corinthians 4:

> Therefore, having this ministry by the mercy of God, we do not lose
> heart. But we have renounced disgraceful, underhanded ways. We
> refuse to practice cunning or to tamper with God's word, but by the
> open statement of the truth we would commend ourselves to every-
> one's conscience in the sight of God. And even if our gospel is veiled,
> it is veiled to those who are perishing. In their case the god of this
> world has blinded the minds of the unbelievers, to keep them from
> seeing the light of the gospel of the glory of Christ, who is the image
> of God. For what we proclaim is not ourselves, but Jesus Christ as
> Lord, with ourselves as your servants for Jesus' sake. For God, who
> said, "Let light shine out of darkness," has shone in our hearts to give
> the light of the knowledge of the glory of God in the face of Jesus
> Christ. (2 Cor. 4:1–6)

This is a dense paragraph theologically, but we are focusing in
this chapter only on the strain of inaugurated eschatology running
through 2 Corinthians. To that end I note the striking way in which
Paul frames salvation in 4:6, where he explicitly casts new realm participation (God shining in our hearts) in terms of the first creation
(God causing primordial light to shine in Gen. 1). Paul's use of the
first creation to speak of salvation in Christ suggests that he views
this salvation as a new creational reality.

This idea is strengthened by two further observations. First, Paul
is going to return to new creation language explicitly in the next
chapter at 2 Corinthians 5:17. Second, Paul likely has in mind not
only Genesis 1 when speaking of light shining in darkness but also
Isaiah 9:1 LXX (9:2 in English versions), which in fact is the only
text in the Septuagint with the exact phrase Paul uses here (*phōs
lampsei*). And Isaiah 9, itself drawing on Genesis 1, is one of the
more richly eschatological texts in the Old Testament. Paul is likely

bringing together both Genesis 1 and Isaiah 9 to speak of Christian salvation as a new creational reality.

The Day of Salvation (6:2 in the Context of 6:1–2)

After Paul speaks of the ministry of reconciliation and the fact that those who are united to Christ find themselves part of the new creation, the apostle pleads with the Corinthians "not to receive the grace of God in vain" (2 Cor. 6:1). But why? The specific grounding that Paul gives is nothing less than the new creational realm in which he and the Corinthians were now living:

> For he says,
>
> > "In a favorable time I listened to you,
> >   and in a day of salvation I have helped you."
>
> Behold, now is the favorable time; behold, now is the day of salvation. (2 Cor. 6:2)

Paul quotes Isaiah 49:8, the context of which is God's assurance of Israel that he will deliver them despite their waywardness. Isaiah goes on to elaborate on the promised future blessings that will flow to God's people:

> Thus says the LORD:
>
> > "In a time of favor I have answered you;
> >   in a day of salvation I have helped you;
> > I will keep you and give you
> >   as a covenant to the people,
> > to establish the land,
> >   to apportion the desolate heritages,
> > saying to the prisoners, 'Come out,'
> >   to those who are in darkness, 'Appear.'

They shall feed along the ways;
> on all bare heights shall be their pasture;
they shall not hunger or thirst,
> neither scorching wind nor sun shall strike them,
for he who has pity on them will lead them,
> and by springs of water will guide them.
And I will make all my mountains a road,
> and my highways shall be raised up." (Isa. 49:8–11)

The striking thing is not so much what Paul quotes but what he then immediately goes on to say of this text from Isaiah 49: "Behold, now is the favorable time; behold, now is the day of salvation" (2 Cor. 6:2). Paul is claiming that the longed-for day of which Isaiah 49 speaks had arrived in the first century. Ridderbos makes the point elegantly in expounding 2 Corinthians 6:2: "Nothing less is intended than that the decisive, long-expected coming of God has dawned, the hour of hours, the day of salvation in the fulfilling, eschatological sense of the word."[23]

This text is not in the first instance exhorting evangelistic zeal when it speaks of today being the day of salvation, though that is a legitimate extrapolating application. The text is building on the notion of new creation (5:17) and asserting that those experiencing the righteousness of God (5:21), union with Christ (5:17), and reconciliation with God (5:18–19) find themselves living in the latter days promised in Isaiah 49.

The Temple of the Living God (6:16 in the Context of 6:14–7:1)

After speaking of the dawning of the "day of salvation" (i.e., the new creational realm), Paul enumerates the labors of his apostolic ministry (6:3–10) and then exhorts the Corinthians to avoid being yoked with unbelievers (6:14–7:1). While it might at first seem that 6:14–7:1 is a

---

23 Ridderbos, *Paul*, 45. Similarly Leonhard Goppelt, *The Variety and Unity of the Apostolic Witness to Christ*, vol. 2 of *Theology of the New Testament*, trans. J. E. Alsup (Grand Rapids, MI: Eerdmans, 1982), 59–60; Gaffin, *In the Fullness of Time*, 269–72.

distraction and irrelevant digression from the broader flow of Paul's argument, in fact it is perfectly fitting if we bear in mind the latent substructure of inaugurated eschatology. The Corinthians have been operating according to the mindset of the old realm, with its focus on outward impressiveness. Paul, therefore, catalogs the way his own ministry has borne marks of both "honor and dishonor" (6:8), and *both* sides of that equation validate new realm ministry (as will become especially clear in chapters 10–13). He then exhorts the Corinthians to beware of falling back into the mindset of the old realm, with all its worldly patterns of thinking; rather, they should "not be unequally yoked with unbelievers" (6:14).

And once more we sit up and take notice at the grounding Paul gives for this ethical injunction, for his reasoning is again the dawning now in the middle of history of the eschaton that was anticipated by Old Testament believers to happen at the end of history.

The overarching eschatological reality that Paul claims as buoying his exhortation is that Christian believers "are the temple of the living God" (6:16). That in itself is an eschatological claim. Paul is not saying that New Testament believers are "like a temple";[24] he is claiming that we are the final temple-to-end-all-temples, the truest and deepest fulfillment of all that was taking place in the Old Testament temples: the presence of God among his people. We no longer enter a temple to meet with God. God has made us into his own temple and is indwelling us so that we ourselves, as believers, have become the eschatological temple. All that the tabernacle and the temple were seeking to capture— restored fellowship with God—has been accomplished in the new age. In Eden, God and man dwelt in harmony. With sin, that fellowship broke and God retreated. The tabernacle, however, was a miniature garden of Eden—complete with a sky-blue ceiling and a lampstand decorated like a flourishing tree (Ex. 25:31–26:37). Eden and then the tabernacle and temple were tangible, physical locations where the im-

---

24 Contra C. K. Barrett, *The Second Epistle to the Corinthians*, BNTC (Peabody, MA: Hendrickson, 1973), 202.

mortal met the mortal, where the supernatural and the natural collided, where the eternal and the temporal intersected, where the sacred and the profane stood face-to-face. The temple was where the divine and the fleshly could meet—never to mix, but to come into brief contact with one another. It was where God dwelt (cf. 2 Cor. 6:16). Rumbling through the Old Testament was the development of the theme of the presence of God among his people, a presence centered in the most sacred of Jewish places, the tabernacle and then the temple. But at the center of all human history, the divine and the fleshly did mix: "And the Word became flesh and tabernacled [eskēnōsen] among us" (John 1:14, my translation; cf. 2:19–22). And then those united to Christ by faith become part of that living temple (Eph. 2:19–22).[25]

Paul's claim in 2 Corinthians 6 that Christians are the end-time temple of God reflects a substructure of inaugurated eschatology for at least three reasons.

First, Paul's broader theology consistently speaks of the church as the eschatological temple of God (1 Cor. 3:16–17; 6:19–20; Eph. 2:19–22).[26]

Second, we find the phrase "of the living God" (theou zōntos) one other time in 2 Corinthians, namely, in 3:3 as Paul draws on Ezekiel 36 to claim that the Corinthians "are a letter from Christ delivered by us, written not with ink but with the Spirit of the living God, not on tablets of stone but on tablets of human hearts."[27] There we find this language of "the living God" explicitly associated with the dawning new realm anticipated by Ezekiel 36 and with the Holy Spirit, which as we will see is a key defining mark of the dawning of the new realm.

Third, returning to the text at hand, the Old Testament passages that Paul then immediately brings to bear on his claim that the church is the latter-day temple of God underscores the eschatological significance of this portion of 2 Corinthians 6. We do not have space to go into a

---

25 In this paragraph and in a few that follow below, I have adapted sections of Ortlund, *2 Corinthians*, 488–90. Used by permission.

26 See G. K. Beale, *The Temple and the Church's Mission: A Biblical Theology of the Dwelling Place of God*, NSBT 17 (Downers Grove, IL: InterVarsity Press, 2004), 245–68.

27 Paul Barnett, *The Second Epistle to the Corinthians*, NICNT (Grand Rapids, MI: Eerdmans, 1997), 350–51.

full exegesis of these texts.[28] But we must note with interest that Paul thoughtfully (if imprecisely with regard to wording) stitches together a catena of several Old Testament texts to insist to the Corinthians that true believers find themselves living in the long-anticipated new realm. The particular proof of this at this point in Paul's argument is that the Corinthian believers are themselves the templing presence of God. It is this theme of the presence of God that draws Paul back to Leviticus 26:12, which forms the first part of the constellation of Old Testament quotes in 2 Corinthians 6:16–18. Throughout the Old Testament, God promises that he will be his people's God and they his people, a promise clearly anticipated in the tabernacle/temple but that burst onto the scene in the coming of Christ, where presence with God was truly accomplished. That God "dwelling among" his people is a temple reality is made clear by examining the immediate context of Leviticus 26, where God says, "I will make my dwelling [lit. 'tabernacle'; Hebrew *mishkan*] among you" (Lev. 26:11).

In 2 Corinthians 6:17 Paul transitions from a text in Leviticus to one in Isaiah, perhaps deliberately tying together both the Law and the Prophets to underscore the whole Old Testament nature of his point about the temple and the presence of God. He cites Isaiah 52:11, and we remember that throughout 2 Corinthians 5–7 Paul is drawing on Isaiah 40–55 to argue that the Corinthians and all believers (whether Jew or Gentile) are the true people of God. Specifically, Isaiah 52:11 is a call for God's people to come out from Babylon and return to Jerusalem. Paul thus takes a text that originally applied to Israel's return from exile and applies it to the Corinthians' situation to call them to dissociate not geographically but spiritually from the paganism around them.

The last line of 2 Corinthians 6:17 ("then I will welcome [*eisdechomai*] you") is drawn not from Isaiah but from Ezekiel 20:34 LXX, where God promises to "gather" (*eisdechomai*) his people out of the nations among whom they are exiled and scattered. This return from exile theme is

---

28   For that I refer the reader to Beale, *Temple and the Church's Mission*, 253–56, or to Barnett, *Second Epistle to the Corinthians*, 351–55.

viewed in Isaiah 40–55 as a second exodus event and hooks into the Leviticus 26 text, which is a promise of God's presence following the first exodus.

Throughout this constellation of Old Testament quotes, then, Paul is melding two major whole-Bible themes: the return from exodus/ exile, and the temple. These reflect the land promise and the divine-presence promise of the original call of Abraham (Gen. 12:1–3). Even in Isaiah 52:11, which speaks of return from exile, the temple theme is not absent: the verse goes on immediately to identify who is to "go out": "you who bear the vessels of the LORD" (Isa. 52:11)—that is, the priests of the temple. But notice what Paul does in 2 Corinthians. He applies this statement, made originally to Israel, to the Gentile Corinthians. Paul understands the Corinthians to be fulfilling the promise made to ethnic Israel in Isaiah 52. This fits with Paul's overarching point that the new realm has broken in on the Corinthians. Consequently, how could they live as if they still belonged to the old realm?

In 2 Corinthians 6:18 Paul concludes by drawing on a high point of Old Testament redemptive history: God's promise to David (among other promises) to be a father to him (2 Sam. 7:14). While Hebrews 1:5 speaks of Christ himself as the fulfillment of this promise, Paul is apply-ing the Davidic promise to the Corinthians. This can be so only when we bear in mind the hermeneutical presupposition of corporate solidarity. Christ is the fulfillment of the Davidic hope, but those who are in Christ become coheirs of that fulfillment by virtue of their union with and representation by Christ. Given the presence of texts from Isaiah 40–55 throughout these middle chapters of 2 Corinthians, it is likely that we should understand Paul's reference to God's "sons and daughters" to be picking up Isaiah 43:6: "Bring my sons from afar / and my daughters from the end of the earth." This is, like Isaiah 52:11 and Ezekiel 20:34, a context in which God is speaking of returning his people from exile and using exodus categories to do so (see esp. Isa. 43:2–3).

Before leaving the temple theme we must note in passing one more text from 2 Corinthians, this time toward the end of the epistle. In Paul's famous thorn-in-the-flesh passage, which we will consider at greater length in the final chapter of this volume, he says, "I will boast all the more gladly of my weaknesses, so that the power of Christ may rest upon me [*episkēnōsē ep' eme*]" (12:9). The use of the verb *episkēnoō* here is arresting as this is tabernacling language. The glory of God rested upon the tabernacle in days of old, the days of the old realm. Now that Christ has come and launched the new realm, God's power—wonder of wonders—rests upon us *directly*, and yet not in the way we would expect. It rests upon weakness. More attention needs to be given to this passage later in this volume, but for now note the repeated use of tabernacle/temple language in 2 Corinthians as signaling the dawn of the latter days, the final eschaton, the new realm.[29]

The Signs of a True Apostle (12:12 in the Context of 12:11–13)

In 2 Corinthians 12 Paul is continuing to reestablish his apostolic legitimacy vis-à-vis the fraudulent impressiveness of the super-apostles. In the course of this defense he reminds the Corinthians that "the signs of a true apostle were performed among you with utmost patience, with signs and wonders and mighty works" (12:12).

Some of us reading this today are immediately thrown into the question of whether these signs were meant to continue beyond the first century or not. But it is beside the point to ask whether these signs continue today; either way, we can all agree that in Paul's day these were signs of the dawning new age. For in these self-attesting apostolic demonstrations we are drawn back to the "signs and wonders" of the exodus event (Ex. 3:20; 7:3; 10:1–2; Num. 14:22; Deut. 4:34; Josh. 24:17). Later Old Testament writers likewise speak of the exodus as a demonstration of "signs and wonders" (e.g., Ps. 105:27 in the context of 105:26–36), and the New Testament too reflects on the exodus as a liberation accompanied by "wonders and signs" (Acts 7:36).

---

29 We have now seen the themes of new covenant (2 Cor. 3), new creation (2 Cor. 5), and new temple (2 Cor. 6) in the letter—three of the five themes that Dumbrell viewed as capturing the basic biblical storyline (the other two being new Israel and new Jerusalem). William J. Dumbrell, *The End of the Beginning: Revelation 21–22 and the Old Testament* (Eugene, OR: Wipf and Stock, 2001).

Just as 2 Corinthians 5–7 draws on Isaiah 40–55, then, and teaches that salvation in Christ is the new and final exodus, so here we see a briefer signal that in the generation of Paul and the apostles the new and final exodus has been launched. The miracles performed by God through Paul were not merely proofs of divine power to validate Paul's ministry—they were, in addition to this and transcending it, a demonstration that the new realm longed for throughout the Old Testament had dawned in the first century.

He Lives by the Power of God (13:4 in the Context of 13:2–4)

We could say much exegetically about 2 Corinthians 13:4. Beginning partway through 13:3, we read that Christ "is not weak in dealing with you, but is powerful among you. For he was crucified in weakness, but lives by the power of God. For we also are weak in him, but in dealing with you we will live with him by the power of God" (13:3–4). Disciplining ourselves to consider only what the text offers with regard to inaugurated eschatology, we note the way that Paul organically connects both the weakness of Christ and believers as well as the power of Christ and believers.

First-century Christians with an underdeveloped sense of the dawning new realm of which they are a part might track with the notion that "we also are weak in him." But what about this idea, apparently equally true, that "we will live with him by the power of God"? As is generally the case in Paul's letters, when he speaks of "life" and "living" he is referring not to living as humans on the earth in some generic way but specifically to the resurrection life of the age to come. Some will note that Paul seems to speak of this resurrection existence as future ("we will live with him"). But the context suggests that the text be read as a gnomic future, speaking of what is broadly true now.[30] In other words, Paul is saying, "We are weak, as those united to a weak Christ—but it is also just as certain that we will simultaneously experience the power of

30 Cf. Daniel B. Wallace, *Greek Grammar beyond the Basics: An Exegetical Syntax of the New Testament* (Grand Rapids, MI: Zondervan, 1996), 571.

resurrection life as well, even now." If Paul were referring to the future when he says, "We will live with him by the power of God," it would hardly make sense for why this is a relevant point in speaking of his imminent visit to the Corinthians, a visit that Paul is claiming will involve not only Christian weakness but also Christian power. Moreover, Paul has already in the previous chapter overlaid divine weakness and strength as simultaneous in the human experience: "*When* I am weak, *then* I am strong" (12:10).

In sum, 2 Corinthians 13:4 reflects the same logic as is laid out at length in 1 Corinthians 15: the resurrection of Christ and the resurrection of believers are both mutually bound up with one another. The added element in 2 Corinthians 13 is that this logic is filtered through a power-through-weakness rubric.

Conclusion

The purpose of this opening chapter has been twofold. First, I explained what is meant by inaugurated eschatology. Second, I positioned 2 Corinthians as a document that is itself written with a lens of inaugurated eschatology and that, therefore, requires its readers to use that same lens if they are to understand it deeply. We considered several texts in which inaugurated eschatology explicitly surfaces, evidencing a pervasive substructure to the letter of a Pauline conviction that the new creational realm has dawned.

In the chapters that follow we will bear in mind the framework or context of inaugurated eschatology as we pursue individual theological themes that are prominent in the letter. We begin with Jesus Christ.

2

Jesus Christ

The Launcher of New Realm Ministry

IT IS ONLY RIGHT THAT, after reflecting at some length on the dawn of the eschaton in 2 Corinthians, we immediately hasten on to consider Jesus Christ, for he is the one in and through whom this new chapter of human history ignited. Just as the inauguration of a new "realm" necessarily involves the coming of a new King to rule that realm, so the new realm as the prophets foretold necessarily involves the coming of Jesus Christ.

In this chapter we proceed in three steps. We'll first consider Christ as the launcher of the new age generally. Second, we will look at how Paul speaks of Jesus in 2 Corinthians specifically. Third, we'll consider how Paul speaks of Christian ministry and life in connection to Jesus in 2 Corinthians, as this is the particular contribution of this epistle— an exploration into what it looks like to do ministry and life joined to the Christ who has launched the new realm.

Jesus Christ and Human History

We can very easily understate the glory and wonder of what dawned in human history when Jesus was born, lived, died, and especially was resurrected; but we cannot overstate it. The following reflections on Christ as the launcher of the new realm could easily balloon into a whole volume on its own, but I must restrict myself to sketching out a few main lines of thought before hurrying on to how 2 Corinthians itself reflects the biblical-theological significance of Jesus Christ.

It is important to get clear on the new realm that Christ brought two thousand years ago because despite the resurgence in biblical-theological reflection in biblical studies and institutions of advanced learning, my experience is that in our churches we continue to remain largely underdeveloped in appreciating just what dawned two thousand years ago. Dispensationalism, while past its heyday, continues to influence the church to look to the future for Old Testament prophecies to be fulfilled, not fully appreciating all that has been fulfilled already in an inaugurated way. And many believers not influenced by dispensationalism nevertheless view Christ's first coming in an eschatologically impoverished way, seeing it as a major event that provides them with forgiveness, but not seeing all that Christ's coming means in terms of the new realm to which they now belong.

To withdraw Jesus from the biblical storyline is not to remove one particularly important figure, even the most important—like removing the most impressive portrait from a room full of portraits of historical figures. No, to remove Jesus is to turn the lights off in the entire room. He is not only the most significant and looming person in Scripture but also the light that illumines everything, the key that unlocks it all—he gives macro-hermeneutical illumination to the whole Bible. Jesus is "the focal point that gathers all the rays of light that issue from Scripture."[1] Perhaps, then, a more accurate description than "Christocentric" as a hermeneutic for reading Scripture would be "Christophotic," as Christ is not so much the "center" of Scripture but the "light" (Greek, *phōs*) that illumines the whole.[2]

---

1   Leonhard Goppelt, *Typos: The Typological Interpretation of the Old Testament in the New*, trans. D. Madvig (Grand Rapids, MI: Eerdmans, 1982), 58.

2   What Lewis beautifully said of how Christianity illumines all of reality, then, I am transposing specifically onto how Christ illumines all of Scripture: "I believe in Christianity as I believe that the Sun has risen, not only because I see it, but because by it I see everything else." C. S. Lewis, "Is Theology Poetry?" in *The Weight of Glory and Other Addresses* (New York: Touchstone, 1996), 106.

But there is more. That Christ is the main point and unlocking key to the whole Bible is a commonly embraced hermeneutical axiom both within and without evangelicalism. This is so in our time perhaps more so than in any previous generation, thanks in part to the rise of the biblical theology movement over the past three generations or so. And we see this kind of Christocentrism (or Christophotism) clearly in the specific teaching of Christ himself (Luke 24:25–27, 44–47; John 1:45; 5:39–47). The specific point we are pursuing right now, however, is the way in which Jesus launched the new realm. How do we understand Christ as the decisive inaugurator of the new creation age that the Old Testament foretold?

We can view the matter in two ways, and on both counts the New Testament speaks with one voice: the teaching of Jesus himself in the Gospels and the teaching of the apostles *about* Jesus in the rest of the New Testament. I will give just a few examples of each.

A key observation with regard to the Gospels is the way in which Jesus speaks of the latter days having arrived in himself. In John 5, for example, Jesus says that anyone who believes in him "has eternal life" and "has passed from death to life" (John 5:24). Jesus will momentarily go on to speak of the future resurrection of both the good and the evil (John 5:28–29), but notice that he also speaks just prior to this (John 5:24–25) of believers experiencing resurrection "life" *now*: "I say to you, an hour is coming, *and is now here*" (John 5:25). Not only the "now" language (we remember the "now" of 2 Cor. 6:2 discussed above) but also the language of the "hour" is of eschatological import, for Jesus is picking up the prophecy of Daniel 12:1–2, which speaks of the coming hour in which the dead will rise to resurrection existence and experience eternal life. Thus, while a final bodily resurrection awaits believers (and unbelievers), that final resurrection has already been launched back into the first century and taken decisive root.[3] We see this language of the eschatological "hour" having arrived in Christ's

---

3   Readers who wish to pursue this further should consult G. K. Beale, *New Testament Biblical Theology: The Unfolding of the Old Testament in the New* (Grand Rapids, MI: Baker Academic, 2011), 129–36.

ministry elsewhere, such as John 4:23 (cf. 1 John 2:18). In Jesus, the latter-day kingdom, the new realm, has—in disguise, so to speak—arrived on the scene of world history.

Turning to the epistles, the evidence becomes even more replete that Jesus is the launcher of the new realm. In 1 Corinthians 10:11 Paul speaks of first-century saints as those "on whom the end of the ages [*ta telē tōn aiōnōn*] has come." This passing but pregnant phrase is deeply revealing of the macro-hermeneutical lens with which Paul reads Scripture and understands world history. For both Judaism and for the apostles, the world was divided into two basic "ages" or "aeons" (cf. the use of *aiōn* in 1 Cor. 10:11 above, which we will see again in 2 Corinthians). We see this distinction between "this age" and "the age to come" in the pages of the New Testament (e.g., Matt. 12:32; Mark 10:30; Luke 18:30; 20:34; Eph. 1:21; Heb. 6:5), and especially in 1 Corinthians (1:20; 2:6, 8; 3:18). The great distinguishing perspective between Judaism and Christianity, however, is that Judaism still awaits the arrival of the age to come, whereas the overarching conviction of the apostles is that the age to come has already arrived. The current age continues on, but for those united to Christ, their basic identity is now in the age to come. This is what we see in 1 Corinthians 10:11, as Paul places himself and his Corinthian readers among those who find themselves belonging to the age to come. The finality of this age to come is underscored in this text by Paul's use of *telos*-language—we are those "on whom the *end* of the ages has come."

Other texts could be adduced to make the same basic point that Jesus, in his life, death, and especially resurrection, opened up the new age or new realm right in the middle of history. Paul opens Galatians by saying that Christ has delivered us "from the present evil age [*aiōn*]" (Gal. 1:4), relocating those united to Christ within the new realm that Christ began. When Paul says that Christ came "in the fullness of time" (Gal. 4:4, briefly discussed in the previous chapter), he doesn't mean mainly that Christ arrived at a particularly strategic point in human history; he is referring to *the* high point of all of human history, the arrival of the long-awaited Jewish Messiah in the middle of history rather than at the end, launching the new age of the Spirit (Gal. 4:6). In Ephesians Paul speaks of God setting forth his supreme divine purpose "in Christ as a plan for the fullness of time, to unite all things in him, things in heaven and things on earth" (Eph. 1:9–10). Paul then goes on to speak of the Father seating Christ in heaven, "far above all rule and authority and power and dominion, and above every name that is named, not only in this age but also in the one to come" (Eph. 1:21). The rhetorical accent is that Christ is supreme even over powers in the age to come, but we note with interest that en route to making this point, Paul speaks of Christ being supreme over every power now in this age. Hebrews 6:5 speaks of those today who "have tasted the goodness of the word of God and the powers of the age to come."

The witness of the New Testament is that Jesus launched the latter-day new realm.

Jesus Christ in 2 Corinthians

The figure of Jesus Christ features prominently throughout 2 Corinthians, "Jesus" occurring fifteen times and "Christ" forty-three times (often together), not counting the many places where he is referred to in the generic third person ("he"/"him"). We are considering the theology of 2 Corinthians and, therefore, could work through each one of these uses and see how orthodox convictions regarding the person and work of Jesus are reflected and reinforced throughout 2 Corinthians: the relationship of Christ to God the Father in 1:2, for example, or the "love of Christ" in 5:14, or union with Christ in 12:2. As Handley C. G. Moule put it in commenting on 2 Corinthians, "Christ *overflows* everywhere into what Paul says."[4] While we will touch on various aspects of the theology of Jesus Christ throughout 2 Corinthians in the course of this volume, I would like to focus on the way in which Christ is presented in 2 Corinthians as launching the new realm, in accord with the brief review of the New Testament generally that we have just concluded.

---

4   Handley C. G. Moule, *The Second Epistle to the Corinthians: A Translation, Paraphrase, and Exposition* (London: Pickering and Inglis, 1962), 8 (emphasis in original).

All the Promises of God

The key passage is the somewhat mysteriously laconic 2 Corinthians 1:20, the key part of which is underlined in its immediate context:

> For the Son of God, Jesus Christ, whom we proclaimed among you, Silvanus and Timothy and I, was not Yes and No, but in him it is always Yes. For all the promises of God find their Yes in him. That is why it is through him that we utter our Amen to God for his glory. And it is God who establishes us with you in Christ, and has anointed us, and who has also put his seal on us and given us his Spirit in our hearts as a guarantee. (2 Cor. 1:19–22)

Amid defending his travel plans, Paul makes the unexpected move in 1:19 of associating his own non-vacillating plans with the non-vacillating way in which Jesus fulfills all of God's promises. The connection between these two is not immediately evident, but we will focus on what Paul says in 1:20 as a way of drawing out Paul's eschatological understanding of Jesus in 2 Corinthians. In the next chapter of this book, we will consider the importance of what Paul says about the Spirit in 1:22.

The key text is the simple sentence in 1:20: "All the promises of God find their Yes in him." It would be difficult to find a text whose brief length is in such disproportionate relationship to its soaring meaning. Paul gathers up virtually the entire Old Testament and locates its clinching fulfillment in the single person of Jesus Christ. But what does it mean?

Let's consider the flow of thought starting in 2 Corinthians 1:19. Paul calls Christ the "Son of God" at various key points in his letters (e.g., 1 Cor. 1:9; Gal. 2:20; Eph. 4:13), though perhaps not as often as one might expect. Given the context, in which Paul asserts Christ as the fulfillment of God's promises, he likely has in mind Christ's role as the great Davidic son anticipated throughout the Old Testament. Particularly significant are the divine promises to David in 2 Samuel 7 that

God would raise up the "offspring" of David and give him a permanent "kingdom," along with God's declaration, "I will be to him a father, and he shall be to me *a son*" (2 Sam. 7:12–14). This coming one would be not only David's son but also, more deeply, God's. This filial motif is carried through the Psalms, with Psalm 2 being especially formative in the apostles' understanding of Jesus's sonship.[5]

How did the Son of God come to be present in the Corinthians (the preposition translated "among" is the same one used to speak of being "in" Christ [e.g., 2 Cor. 2:14])? Not by paraded example, not by acts of kindness, not even by written letter such as Paul is now writing to them—but by oral proclamation. The text woodenly reads that Christ is in/among the Corinthians "through what was preached by us"—that is, preaching was the means by which Christ came to Corinth, but preaching was not the original source. The proclamation came *through* Paul and his comrades. This is perhaps why Paul has used the passive ("was preached"). It came from a source higher up still—from heaven, from God himself. As Paul will say later of his ministry, "All this is from God" (2 Cor. 5:18).

Paul then makes what is perhaps, on first reading, a strange remark. The proclaimed Christ "was not Yes and No, but in him it is always Yes" (1:19). What Paul is getting at is that the very integrity of God has been publicly vindicated in the explosion onto the scene of world history of God's great "Yes" in the person of his Son. God hasn't declared "Maybe" to sinners. He has said *yes* to them, wholeheartedly and unreservedly. All the snowballing assurances throughout the Old Testament of God's care for his people have been decisively and irreversibly clinched in the outwardly unimpressive carpenter from Nazareth (cf. Luke 24:27, 44; John 5:39, 46; Rom. 1:2–3; 9:4–5; 15:8).

We know this mindfulness of the Old Testament is the point because Paul goes on in the next verse to ground what he has just said in 2 Corinthians 1:19 (note the connecting "For" that opens 1:20), and

---

5 This paragraph and the few that follow have been adapted from my commentary, Dane Ortlund, *2 Corinthians*, in *Romans–Galatians*, vol. 10 of *ESV Expository Commentary* (Wheaton, IL: Crossway, 2020), 418–19. Used by permission.

he does so by connecting Christ's great "Yes" to "the promises of God" (1:20). And not some of God's promises; "*all* the promises of God find their Yes in him." Literally, "as many as are the promises of God, in him [is] the Yes." Whatever God has pledged, in Christ it is cemented. Whatever God has said he will do, in Christ he has done it. Jesus Christ is flesh-and-blood proof that God is faithful—that is, true to his word.

The glory of what Paul is saying is difficult to capture with words. When Jesus appeared in Palestine in the first century, we were not being given even more certainty that God's ancient promises to his people down through the centuries would one day come true. We were given, in human form, the final proof that *his promises had already now begun to come true.* The Davidic Son, bringing with him the new kingdom or realm, had arrived. One day he would return openly rather than in disguise, but his first coming initiated the longed-for new creational age of which the prophets foretold.

Other Texts in 2 Corinthians

We have focused on 2 Corinthians 1:20 given how rich a text it is for considering Christ as the launcher of the new realm, not only for 2 Corinthians but for the whole New Testament. But other texts in this epistle likewise join in reflecting Christ as the launcher of the new realm. Here we more briefly consider a few of these.

In 3:14 Paul is mid-argument as he correlates Moses to Christ and the respective "veil" associated with each. Without plunging into the whole argument, we note what Paul says in 3:14 and notice specifically what he says about Christ: "But their minds were hardened. For to this day, when they read the old covenant, that same veil remains unlifted, because only through Christ is it taken away." The veil that prevents hardened human hearts from seeing the beauty and glory of Christ (cf. 4:4), associated explicitly in this text with reading "the old covenant," is removed "only through Christ." Jesus Christ is the one who takes believers from old covenant blindness to new covenant vision. Paul depicts Jesus as the one who causes new covenant realities to crack open here and now.

In 4:4 we read that "the god of this world has blinded the minds of the unbelievers, to keep them from seeing the light of the gospel of the glory of Christ, who is the image of God." All we are noting is what the text says of Christ and, in this case, the contrast that is set up between "the god of this world" and Christ and his glory. "This world" is an unfortunate translation because the Greek word is not *kosmos* but *aiōn*, elsewhere rendered "age" and, as we have seen above, referring to "the present evil age" as Galatians 1:4 puts it in distinction from the "age to come."[6] The reference is to Satan in 2 Corinthians 4:4,[7] and the duality Paul is setting up is of Satan as the power representing this age and (implicitly) Jesus as the power representing the age to come. The final added moniker of Jesus as "the image of God" likely underscores his eschatological significance. We see throughout the New Testament the notion that Christ is the true and final Adamic figure, representing and restoring the divine image to humanity (Rom. 8:29; 1 Cor. 15:49; Col. 1:15; cf. 3:9–10). In the immediate context, the allusion to Genesis 1 a few verses later (2 Cor. 4:6) strengthens the probability that "the image of God" has Adamic and thus eschatological undertones in 2 Corinthians 4:4, since elsewhere Paul casts Christ as the last Adam, inaugurating the new humanity in response to Adam's tragic work (Rom. 5:12–19).[8]

We see clearly a new creational motif in 2 Corinthians 4:6 as Paul correlates the first creation in Genesis 1 with the aeon in which we who see Christ clearly find ourselves: "For God, who said, 'Let light shine out of darkness,' has shone in our hearts to give the light of the knowledge of the glory of God in the face of Jesus Christ." Paul reaches all the way back to the third verse of the Bible—"And God said, 'Let there be light,' and there was light" (Gen. 1:3)—to speak of saving association with Christ as a matter of God once again causing light to shine—not, this time, cosmic light in the sky, but spiritual light in our

---

6 *Aiōn* occurs only two other times in 2 Corinthians, but neither is of eschatological significance (9:9; 11:31).

7 We will consider Satan as the great enemy within the new realm in chapter 4.

8 See Beale, *New Testament Biblical Theology*, 445, and the whole section from pp. 438–68 for a defense of the notion that "image" language in the New Testament often refers to restored Adamic (and thus eschatological) dignity.

hearts. In the previous chapter we noted the general way this reference to Genesis 1 puts 2 Corinthians 4:6 in a creation / new creation frame of reference; now we are specifically noting the connection to Christ. In 4:6 Paul speaks of Christ's face by continuing to draw on the Moses/veil motif that had begun in 3:7. Divine glory was reflected on Moses's face, which could not be looked at directly (Ex. 34:29–35); but now divine glory is reflected on Christ's face, which, astonishingly, *can* be looked upon. By speaking of Christ's ministry not only as recapitulating Moses's ministry but also God's creational work, Paul continues to present Jesus as the one in whom the new age, the new realm, rises on world history.

In 2 Corinthians 4:7–12, we continue to see evidence that in Jesus the new and final realm has opened up on world history. The point to note is the way in which Paul speaks of both the death of Jesus and the resurrection life of Jesus as overlaid realities here and now—as opposed to believers experiencing the death of Jesus now and waiting to experience his resurrection life only in the future. No, "we who live are always being given over to death for Jesus' sake, so that the life of Jesus also may be manifested in our mortal flesh" (4:11). Those in union with Christ experience resurrection life *now* (the life of the new realm) even in this mortal existence (the old realm).

And of course we must mention in closing 5:17: "Therefore, if anyone is in Christ, he is a new creation. The old has passed away; behold, the new has come." Here we simply note that this new realm comes *in Christ.* He brings it. And we sinners are swept into that new realm as we are united to Christ ("if anyone is *in* Christ").

I have been seeking to show that throughout 2 Corinthians, most notably at 1:20 but also elsewhere, Jesus is presented as the launcher of the new realm. All this is not to say that there is no remaining future consummation. In 2 Corinthians 1:14 Paul expresses confidence "that on the day of our Lord Jesus you will boast of us as we will boast of you." This clearly refers to the future time when Jesus returns to earth. But this is the minor note in speaking of Christ in 2 Corinthians; the major note is what has already transpired in our space and time history with the first coming of Jesus as he inaugurated the age to come overlaid with the already existing present age.

Christian Life and Ministry in Light of Christ's Launching the New Realm

Having considered Jesus as the launcher of the new realm in the New Testament broadly and also the same truth in 2 Corinthians specifically, we close by funneling down even further to the apostles' (and derivatively our own) connection to these realities.

With one of the texts considered immediately above we already began to see the close intertwining of Christ with his followers (4:7–11). Other texts in their own way express this joining of Christ and the believer. In chapter 7 of this book, we will look at the most prominent and sustained way in which Christ, the new realm, and the believer are brought together—the theme of strength through weakness. But here and there along the way, it will be useful to draw attention explicitly, if briefly, to the ways in which Paul's life, the Corinthians' lives, and our own lives today reflect the eschatological realities we are seeing in 2 Corinthians. Let's look at three representative texts.

Consider 1:21 first. Just after his towering assertion that all of God's promises find their home in Jesus (1:20), Paul says, "And it is God who establishes us with you in Christ, and has anointed us" (1:21). The apostle is saying that he is bound together with the Corinthians in co-union with Christ ("with you in Christ") and that this was not due to any human ingenuity or worldly strategy but from God himself ("it is God who establishes us"). Already we feel the weight of the solidarity between Christ and believers. But then notice the audacity of the final phrase: "and has anointed us." This would be a shocking thing for any first-century person familiar with Judaism to hear, for the verb is the term that throughout Scripture refers to the anointing of the Davidic Messiah, the coming King who would restore God's people. It is the verb *chriō*, from which we get the Greek noun *Christos* ("anointed one"), coming into English as the transliterated "Christ." It is the Greek equivalent of the Hebrew *Mashiah* ("Messiah"), likewise meaning "anointed one." Christ alone is the Messiah, the anointed Savior; but those in union with him are "co-anointed" with him, not in a co-saving way but in a co-reigning way, as other Pauline texts corroborate (1 Cor. 6:1–3; 2 Tim. 2:12; cf. Rev. 20:6).

Second, we read in 2 Corinthians 2:15 that "we are the aroma of Christ to God among those who are being saved and among those who are perishing." The nature of the relationship between Christ and the believer is so vital (i.e., a matter of joint life) that we not only carry the message of Jesus but also the aroma of Jesus. Those who are being saved by Christ smell us, and they smell life; those who are perishing smell us, and they are hardened into a further state of death (2:16). In the new realm, the King and his subjects are united in such a profound and spiritually organic way that not only the objective content from our lips but the subjective aroma of our lives carries the "air" of this new aeon—oxygenating to believers, asphyxiating to unbelievers.

Third and finally, we note the entire passage running from 5:11 to 6:2. This is a category-creating passage for Christians who wrongly understand Christ to be their substitute only. He is that, to be sure, but he is also our representative head. As our substitute, he goes where we don't, in our place, but as our representative, we follow where he goes. Indeed, we must: we are joined to him. Here's what the text says:

> Therefore, knowing the fear of the Lord, we persuade others. But what we are is known to God, and I hope it is known also to your conscience. We are not commending ourselves to you again but giving you cause to boast about us, so that you may be able to answer those who boast about outward appearance and not about what is in the heart. For if we are beside ourselves, it is for God; if we are in our right mind, it is for you. For the love of Christ controls us, because we have concluded this: that one has died for all, therefore all have died; and he died for all, that those who live might no longer live for themselves but for him who for their sake died and was raised.
>
> From now on, therefore, we regard no one according to the flesh. Even though we once regarded Christ according to the flesh, we regard him thus no longer. Therefore, if anyone is in Christ, he is a

new creation. The old has passed away; behold, the new has come. All this is from God, who through Christ reconciled us to himself and gave us the ministry of reconciliation; that is, in Christ God was reconciling the world to himself, not counting their trespasses against them, and entrusting to us the message of reconciliation. Therefore, we are ambassadors for Christ, God making his appeal through us. We implore you on behalf of Christ, be reconciled to God. For our sake he made him to be sin who knew no sin, so that in him we might become the righteousness of God.

Working together with him, then, we appeal to you not to receive the grace of God in vain. For he says,

"In a favorable time I listened to you,
    and in a day of salvation I have helped you."

Behold, now is the favorable time; behold, now is the day of salvation. (2 Cor. 5:11–6:2)

A text such as this remains opaque unless we understand the ancient hermeneutical principle of *corporate solidarity* (or corporate representation, or, as H. Wheeler Robinson coined it over a century ago, "corporate personality"[9]). We don't naturally think in this way in the twenty-first-century West, so we need to be crystal clear: The ancient mindset, socially speaking, was one in which the leader represented his group. As goes the head, king, judge, or conqueror, so go those who belong to him. This was true of large contexts (king to subjects) right down to the smallest context (father to children; husband to wife). To speak of the leader is to necessarily include the group, and vice versa. To put it simply, the group is "in" the leader—precisely the language we find in the New Testament of believers being "in" Christ.[10]

---

9 H. Wheeler Robinson, *The Christian Doctrine of Man* (Edinburgh: T&T Clark, 1911); H. Wheeler Robinson, *Corporate Personality in Ancient Israel* (Philadelphia: Fortress, 1964).

10 For a clear and useful exploration of the notion of corporate solidarity, see Richard N. Longenecker, *Biblical Exegesis in the Apostolic Period* (Grand Rapids, MI: Eerdmans, 1999), 77–79.

We see this notion of corporate solidarity throughout the Old Testament. Consider for example Isaiah 49:8, which is quoted at the end of the above passage in 2 Corinthians 6:2. Earlier in Isaiah 49 we read,

> The LORD called me from the womb,
> > from the body of my mother he named my name.
> He made my mouth like a sharp sword;
> > in the shadow of his hand he hid me;
> he made me a polished arrow;
> > in his quiver he hid me away.
> And he said to me, "You are my servant,
> > Israel, in whom I will be glorified."
> But I said, "I have labored in vain;
> > I have spent my strength for nothing and vanity;
> yet surely my right is with the LORD,
> > and my recompense with my God."
> And now the LORD says,
> > he who formed me from the womb to be his servant,
> to bring Jacob back to him;
> > and that Israel might be gathered to him—
> for I am honored in the eyes of the LORD,
> > and my God has become my strength—
> he says:
> "It is too light a thing that you should be my servant
> > to raise up the tribes of Jacob
> > and to bring back the preserved of Israel;
> I will make you as a light for the nations,
> > that my salvation may reach to the end of the earth."
> > (Isa. 49:1–6)

The Lord is speaking here in the second of the four Servant Songs. In 49:3 it appears plain that the servant is Israel: "You are my servant, Israel." But shortly thereafter, in 49:6, we read that the servant will himself "raise up the tribes of Jacob and . . . bring back the preserved of Israel." Which is it? Is the servant Israel or the figure who will save Israel? The answer is: both. By the hermeneutical axiom of corporate solidarity, we understand how both can be true. The servant will save Israel—by *becoming* Israel, representatively.

Corporate solidarity works not only salvifically but also punitively. One thinks of the Achan incident, for example, in Joshua 7:10–26, in which Achan alone sins, but his whole family is killed in judgment (Josh. 7:24–25). Indeed, not only Achan's family but the whole nation appears to be included vicariously in the judgment, for the text explicitly reflects on Achan's sin with the statement, "Israel has sinned" (Josh. 7:11). Early Jewish thought explicitly read the fall of Adam in terms of corporate solidarity also (see 4 Ezra 7:118).

What does all this have to do with 2 Corinthians? Much in every way: look at 2 Corinthians 5:14 and the built-up literary force as Paul says, "We have concluded this: that one has died for all, therefore all have died." For a Christian who understands Christ's death only as vicarious substitute, this statement will be mystifying. But Christ's death has two aspects: both substitution and representation.[11] He stands in for believers in the first; but believers join him in the second. If we are in Christ, we have died. His crucifixion is ours so that, freed from the penalty of sin, believers "might no longer live for themselves but for him who for their sake died and was raised" (5:15).

We continue to see the corporate solidarity that believers and Christ share in the new realm throughout this passage. Paul goes on to speak of the ministry of reconciliation and once more tightly binds the exclusive reconciling work of Christ with the summoned partnership of believers in that reconciling work: God "through Christ reconciled us to himself [exclusive] and gave us the ministry of reconciliation [representative]" (5:18). In the work of Christ, God was not only "reconciling the

---

11 Wright speaks of Christ as both our "representative" and "substitute" and rightly sees the two as "inextricably united." N. T. Wright, "The Challenge of Dialogue: A Partial and Preliminary Response," in *God and the Faithfulness of Paul: A Critical Examination of the Pauline Theology of N. T. Wright*, ed. C. Heilig, J. T. Hewitt, and M. F. Bird (Minneapolis: Fortress, 2017), 734, though the latter notion (substitution) is less robustly upheld in Wright's work than the former (representation).

world to himself [exclusively]" but also "entrusting to us the message of reconciliation [representatively]" (5:19). Paul's conclusion is plain: "Therefore, we are ambassadors for Christ, God making his appeal through us" (5:20). An ambassador is a citizen of one realm who is living in another realm yet who most truly belongs to and represents his homeland. Here we see the inaugurated eschaton clearly: we are citizens of the new realm (the "new creation" as Paul puts it a few verses earlier in 5:17), representing Christ, the beginner of that new realm, in the "foreign territory" of this fallen world and the old realm in which we find ourselves living.

Given what we are seeing of corporate solidarity throughout 2 Corinthians 5, it is not surprising that Paul opens 2 Corinthians 6 with the following words: "Working together with him, then." Christ[12] has deigned to summon us into the ministry of the new realm, proclaiming the gospel of divinely provided reconciliation as we also give off the very aroma of this glorious message (2:15). And this co-laboring with God is grounded (note the "For" that opens 6:2) in the dawning new day of world history, the "day of salvation" that Isaiah prophesied and that has now erupted on the world scene. This grand event has taken place, we have observed throughout this chapter, *in Jesus Christ*.

In the preceding paragraphs, we have looked at three texts in 2 Corinthians in which the believer and Christ are closely aligned as sharing in the same new realm existence that Christ launched. This fits with the broader aim of this chapter to consider how Paul speaks of Jesus in 2 Corinthians. We have focused on the thrilling truth that Jesus launched the new creational realm. Those united to Jesus share in both the death and the resurrection life that in Christ's own experience were the launching pad for this new realm, and we now co-labor with him to bring to the world the message of this new creation that his reconciling work wrought.

Some readers may wonder why I have said little in this chapter about the atoning *work* of Christ, which in 2 Corinthians is cast as God

---

12   The "him" of 6:1 likely carries forward the "him" of 5:21, which is Christ.

reconciling sinners to himself (5:18–21). Ralph Martin went so far as to put forth reconciliation as the center of Paul's theology, though few followed him in that.[13] I considered having a section in this chapter on that theological subject, or even giving this subject its own chapter. I ultimately decided it was not needed, for four reasons. First, there is little, relatively speaking, about the work of Christ in 2 Corinthians. The only texts that would be brought to bear on it would be a few verses from 2 Corinthians 5 (5:14, 18–21) and 13:4, which is six verses out of 242 (2.5 percent). Second, in these passages (5:14–21 and 13:4) Christ's death is being brought to bear on a deeper goal in Paul's writing, the texts seeking to veer the Corinthians away from the cliff of a worldly/ fleshly way of thinking (see 5:16; 6:1; 13:2–3). Third, I am seeking in this volume to major on what Paul majors on, and the reconciling work of God in Christ, while a vital theological matter, is not a major theme in 2 Corinthians as is the dawning new age, or strength through weakness, or the Christian relationships that are at play pervasively throughout the letter. Fourth, the work of Christ has received much attention in biblical scholarship in our generation, so bypassing it for more neglected themes seems warranted.

Even if we were to devote a whole section or chapter to reconciliation as a key theological theme in 2 Corinthians, we would continue to be able to underscore the importance of inaugurated eschatology for understanding this letter, as reconciliation is itself the fulfillment to the prophetic hope (esp. from Isa. 40–66) of a restored relationship between God and his people in the new creation.[14]

Having explained my reasons for not spending a significant amount of this book exploring Paul's theology of atonement in 2 Corinthians, I immediately affirm that 2 Corinthians 5 does contribute to our understanding of Paul's atonement theology, and it does that in three

---

13 Ralph P. Martin, *Reconciliation: A Study in Paul's Theology* (London: Marshall, Morgan, and Scott, 1981).

14 On which see G. K. Beale, "The Old Testament Background of Reconciliation in 2 Corinthians 5–7 and Its Bearing on the Literary Problem of 2 Corinthians 4:14–7:1," *NTS* 35, no. 4 (1989): 550–81; Mark Gignilliat, *Paul and Isaiah's Servants: Paul's Theological Reading of Isaiah 40–66 in 2 Corinthians 5:14–6:10*, LNTS (London: T&T Clark, 2007).

particular ways. First, 2 Corinthians 5 underscores our doctrine of sin. Humanity is alienated from God—hence, the need for reconciliation. While justification is the law court image for salvation, sanctification the cultic image, adoption the familial image, and so on, reconciliation is the relational or friendship image. Second, God is, surprisingly, the initiator of this restored friendship. The divine initiative is evident throughout the closing verses of 2 Corinthians 5: "All this is from God" (5:18), "in Christ God was reconciling the world" (5:19), "God making his appeal through us" (5:20). Third, 2 Corinthians 5:21 is one of the clearest biblical affirmations of the classic facet of atonement theology we call *imputation*—Christ was made sin so that we might be made righteous (i.e., accounted righteous for Christ's sake).[15] Believers in Christ receive the righteous status of Jesus himself as Jesus took upon himself the sinful status of believers.

I close this chapter with a soaring reflection from Donald Robinson, a twentieth-century Australian Bible scholar who was also the primary theological mentor to Graeme Goldsworthy. This quote, which Robinson begins with 2 Corinthians 1:20, captures what we have been seeing in 2 Corinthians in this chapter.

> Jesus is Himself the End. There is nothing revealed to us in the purposes of God which does not have its fulfillment in Jesus Christ (2 Cor. 1:20).
>
> All that the Old Testament believers looked forward to in the day of the Lord finds its realization in Jesus: the passover (1 Cor. 5:7), the exodus (Luke 9:31), the covenant (Matt. 26:28), the law (John 13:34; Rom. 10:4), the tabernacle (John 1:14), the bread from heaven (John 6:35), Canaan (1 Pet. 1:4; Heb. 11:16), David (John 1:49), Jerusalem (Heb. 12:22; Rev. 21:10–14), the Temple (John 2:21; Acts 15:16).
>
> But Jesus not only concludes and fulfills the historical experience of old Israel; He fulfills also the more ancient history of creation. He

---

15 The strongest explication of atonement theology I have come across is Donald Macleod, *Christ Crucified: Understanding the Atonement* (Downers Grove, IL: IVP Academic, 2014), who treats 2 Cor. 5:18–21 specifically on 154–58.

is the last Adam (1 Cor. 15:45), the firstborn of all creation (Col. 1:15), who has already received the glory and dominion with which it was God's purpose to endow man (Heb. 2:5–9).

The End has therefore come in Jesus Christ. . . . There is nothing whatever of all God's purposes of salvation which has not been fulfilled in Him.[16]

16 Donald W. B. Robinson, *The Hope of Christ's Coming* (London: Falcon, 1960), 13–14.

3

The Spirit

The Sign of New Realm Ministry

ON FIRST READING, the above chapter title may conjure up for readers notions of extraordinary or miraculous signs from the Holy Spirit to demonstrate the dawning of the new realm. While Paul does appeal to the extraordinary "signs and wonders and mighty works" in 2 Corinthians 12:12, this aspect of the work of the Spirit is not centrally what I mean by designating the Spirit as the sign of new realm ministry. Indeed, there is very little in 2 Corinthians about the gifting or extraordinary manifestations of the Spirit; for that we must go to 1 Corinthians. When it comes to 2 Corinthians, the chapter title above refers to the following thesis: *in tandem with the coming of the Messiah, the descent of the Holy Spirit is the most decisive proof that the new creational realm has dawned.* This eschatological aspect of the Spirit is as strong or stronger in 2 Corinthians than in any other New Testament book. Romans reflects, more than any Pauline letter, on the nature of what life in the Spirit looks like (see Rom. 8:2–27), and Galatians reflects more deeply on the redemptive-historical significance of the Spirit for Gentiles (see Gal. 3:2–5:25 passim). But 2 Corinthians is in first place when it comes to theologically pregnant comments on the Spirit, especially as the Spirit relates to the new realm. A focused chapter on the Spirit is thus merited by this theme's prominence in

2 Corinthians, as well as by a possible neglect of the Spirit in Pauline theology more broadly.[1]

I acknowledge up front the critical insight of Geerhardus Vos in his seminal 1912 essay, "The Eschatological Aspect of the Pauline Conception of the Spirit." Vos reviews texts from the Old Testament, Second Temple Judaism, and supremely the New Testament to argue that the coming of the Spirit was *the* sign that the new realm had begun.[2] This may sound like an overstatement. Isn't the coming of Christ the supreme sign? From one perspective, to be sure. And we would not want to divorce the coming of Christ and the immediately subsequent coming of the Spirit. But as Vos points out, the coming of Christ to earth lasted a few short years, whereas the coming of the Spirit lasts the entire duration of the new age.[3] The Spirit is, as Jesus teaches in John 14–16, the continuation of the presence of Jesus on earth. Moreover, and looking at the first-century events very specifically, it was not Christ's birth or life or death that launched the new realm, though of course the new realm could not be a reality without Christ's coming and ministry in its totality. Rather, the new realm was launched in Christ's resurrection in that this was the first instance of the new kind of humanity, the humanity of the new creational realm. The risen Christ was literally and physically the

---

1 I think not only of an arguable neglect of the Spirit in my own little corner of the Christian church (conservative American Presbyterianism) but also in New Testament study more broadly. For example, James D. G. Dunn, "An Insider's Perspective on Wright's Version of the New Perspective on Paul," in *God and the Faithfulness of Paul: A Critical Examination of the Pauline Theology of N. T. Wright*, ed. C. Heilig, J. T. Hewitt, and M. F. Bird (Minneapolis: Fortress, 2017), 352, strongly rebukes N. T. Wright for neglecting the Spirit (or "spirit" as Wright insists) in Wright's magnum opus *Paul and the Faithfulness of God*, vol. 4 of Christian Origins and the Question of God (Minneapolis: Fortress, 2013).

2 Geerhardus Vos, "The Eschatological Aspect of the Pauline Conception of the Spirit," in *Redemptive History and Biblical Interpretation: The Collected Shorter Writings of Geerhardus Vos*, ed. R. B. Gaffin Jr. (Phillipsburg, NJ: P&R, 1980), 91–125. Other expositors of the Spirit as a vital mark of the dawning eschaton in Paul's theology generally include Finny Philip, *The Origins of Pauline Eschatology: The Eschatological Bestowal of the Spirit upon Gentiles in Judaism and in the Early Development of Paul's Theology*, WUNT 2/194 (Tübingen: Mohr Siebeck, 2005); G. K. Beale, *New Testament Biblical Theology: The Unfolding of the Old Testament in the New* (Grand Rapids, MI: Baker Academic, 2011), 559–650.

3 Vos, "The Eschatological Aspect," 96–97.

beginning of the new realm. Yet, even when Christ was raised, the new realm had not come for the rest of us until the Holy Spirit descended at Pentecost.[4] "The Spirit who has come at Pentecost is the Spirit of the future age," writes Ferguson, so that "the world into which he brings believers is marked by the powers of the aeon to come."[5]

Having said this, we should be careful that we do not overly differentiate these different aspects of Christ's ministry and the coming of the Spirit—Christ's whole ministry (through his ascension) and the coming of the Spirit at Pentecost together comprise a single coherent event-complex, each element bound up inextricably with the others.[6] Another clarification lest I be misunderstood is that I am not proposing in this chapter that there was no operation of the Spirit in the Old Testament. There clearly was. Indeed, in 2 Corinthians 4:13 we see Paul connect the experience of the Spirit in the first century with the psalmist's experience of "the same spirit" (ESV; or, more likely, "the same Spirit").[7] In this chapter I am simply saying that what was sporadically and occasionally experienced in the Old Testament aeon exploded onto the scene of human history with universal and profound depth in the New Testament aeon, reflecting the dawning new realm.

We will proceed in four steps as we consider the Spirit in 2 Corinthians. First, we will consider the two uses of *arrabōn* ("down payment")

---

4   On which see Richard B. Gaffin Jr., *In the Fullness of Time: An Introduction to the Biblical Theology of Acts and Paul* (Wheaton, IL: Crossway, 2022), 119–52, who stresses the unrepeatability and finality of what took place in the descent of the Spirit at Pentecost. Similarly Herman Ridderbos, *Paul: An Outline of His Theology*, trans. John Richard de Witt (Grand Rapids, MI: Eerdmans, 1975), 215.

5   Sinclair B. Ferguson, *The Holy Spirit*, Contours of Christian Theology (Downers Grove, IL: InterVarsity Press, 1996), 119. Despite the occasional comment to this effect, this particular volume is otherwise thin on the Spirit specifically as the evidence that the new aeon has dawned. Throughout the present chapter, I wish to provide an alternate perspective on reality than the claim of John Levison that we had to wait till N. T. Wright to have a Pauline scholar "bring pneumatology into the bloodstream of Pauline theology." John R. Levison, "The Spirit in Its Second Temple Context: An Exegetical Analysis of the Pneumatology of N. T. Wright," in Heilig, Hewitt, and Bird, *God and the Faithfulness of Paul*, 440. Vos had already done that.

6   Cf. Gaffin, *In the Fullness of Time*, 121.

7   Cf. Vos, "The Eschatological Aspect," 100–101.

in 2 Corinthians. Second, we will look at the Spirit in 2 Corinthians 3, where the Spirit is clearly a fulfillment of Old Testament eschatological hope. Third, we will look briefly at a smattering of other uses of Spirit language in 2 Corinthians. Fourth, I will synthesize the findings with a short summary of Paul's theology of the Spirit in 2 Corinthians.

The Spirit as Down Payment (1:22; 5:5)

The first and most important observation is that two of the three New Testament instances of the key word describing the eschatological significance of the Holy Spirit occur in 2 Corinthians. That word is *arrabōn*, and it refers to a down payment, deposit, pledge, or guarantee. It is the first part of a single gift or payment.[8] In all three New Testament uses, it describes the Holy Spirit and is translated by the ESV as "guarantee," underlined below:

> And it is God who establishes us with you in Christ, and has anointed us, and who has also put his seal on us and given us his Spirit in our hearts as a guarantee. (2 Cor. 1:21–22)

> He who has prepared us for this very thing is God, who has given us the Spirit as a guarantee. (2 Cor. 5:5)

> In him you also, when you heard the word of truth, the gospel of your salvation, and believed in him, were sealed with the promised Holy Spirit, who is the guarantee of our inheritance until we acquire possession of it, to the praise of his glory. (Eph. 1:13–14)

The two uses in 2 Corinthians speak of the Spirit being "given" (using the verb *didōmi*), which underscores the divine graciousness of this gift. And the uses in 2 Corinthians 1:22 and Ephesians 1:14 both speak of believers being "sealed" (using the verb *sphragizō*) with this gift of the Spirit, underscoring the unrepeatable and permanent

---

8 "Payment of part of a purchase price in advance." "Ἀρραβών," BDAG 134.

nature of this gift (Paul speaks again in Eph. 4:30 of the Spirit as the agent by whom believers are sealed, though he does not use the term *arrabōn*). But what is most prominent in speaking of the Spirit as the *arrabōn* in these three texts is the eschatological significance of such a denominator.

While "guarantee" is a good translation, we can easily miss all that is meant by the underlying Greek word. An English reader might conclude that some generic notion is meant, as if the Spirit is just one more reassurance from God that everything will turn out well in the end for believers (we often use the word "guarantee" more colloquially—"I guarantee it!"). But the actual content of this word lies far deeper and stitches together the two comings of Christ. In the giving of the Spirit to believers, we are helped to more accurately see the two comings of Christ as two phases of one arrival. I don't want to overstate the matter; Christ indeed comes at two distinct times, once in disguise in our past and once in glory in our future. But these two arrivals are organically connected, and the Spirit as *arrabōn* expresses that organic unity, holding the two comings together.

The descent of the Spirit as *arrabōn* is a parallel reality to the resurrection of Christ as the *aparchē* ("firstfruits") of the resurrection of all believers (1 Cor. 15:20, 23). Here we bear in mind what we saw in chapter 1 about resurrection as the lynchpin to the inauguration of the new realm. Christ's resurrection was the initial ingathering of a single harvest—one great crop, the firstfruits (Christ's bodily resurrection) guaranteeing the inevitable fuller ingathering (believers' bodily resurrection). And *what* aparchē *is to the eschatological significance of the resurrection,* arrabōn *is to the eschatological significance of the Holy Spirit.* The Spirit is the one who creates the spiritual, though real, resurrection in believers now, with the future bodily aspect rendered certain to come.[9]

---

9 In Calvin's otherwise typically masterful handling of 2 Corinthians, this is the one notable weakness—he does not fully see the ways in which Paul is operating with an inaugurated eschatology lens. I explore this in Dane C. Ortlund, "The Text of 1 & 2 Corinthians and the Theology of Calvin," in *Reformation Readings of Paul: Explorations in History and*

The Spirit (New Realm) versus the Letter (Old Realm)

We turn now to 2 Corinthians 3. Having already considered the general undertone of inaugurated eschatology permeating this reflection by Paul that the new covenant has arrived, we now focus more specifically on what Paul says of the Spirit. He mentions the Spirit four times in the first half of the chapter, and the cumulative effect of all four indicates unambiguously that the Spirit is the key agent of life in the new realm:

> Are we beginning to commend ourselves again? Or do we need, as some do, letters of recommendation to you, or from you? You your-selves are our letter of recommendation, written on our hearts, to be known and read by all. And you show that you are a letter from Christ delivered by us, written not with ink but with the Spirit of the living God, not on tablets of stone but on tablets of human hearts.
>
> Such is the confidence that we have through Christ toward God. Not that we are sufficient in ourselves to claim anything as coming from us, but our sufficiency is from God, who has made us sufficient to be ministers of a new covenant, not of the letter but of the Spirit. For the letter kills, but the Spirit gives life.
>
> Now if the ministry of death, carved in letters on stone, came with such glory that the Israelites could not gaze at Moses' face because of its glory, which was being brought to an end, will not the ministry of the Spirit have even more glory? (2 Cor. 3:1–8)

In 3:1–6 Paul is defending his validity as a minister, and he does so by speaking of the Corinthians themselves as the "letter of recom-mendation" that would normally be needed to ratify someone such as Paul. But Paul plunges the notion of a commendation letter deep into the Corinthians themselves, describing them as the letter, Christ as the author of the letter, Paul as the deliverer of the letter, the human heart as the tablet on which the letter is written, and—most crucially

---

Exegesis, ed. M. Allen and J. A. Linebaugh (Downers Grove, IL: IVP Academic, 2015), 187–208, esp. 205–8.

for this chapter of our study—the Holy Spirit as the ink with which the letter is written: "written not with ink but with the Spirit of the living God" (3:3).[10]

But at this point Paul is doing more than simply referring to the Corinthians as his living letters of ministerial justification. He is placing his ministry among the Corinthians in the context of the full sweep of redemptive history. In describing the Corinthians as letters Paul is not only saying, "Don't you know *what* you are?" but also saying, "Don't you know *when* you are? Do you not recognize what era of world history you find yourselves in?"[11] With his cascade of metaphors for describing the Corinthians as living letters, Paul is drawing on a constellation of key Old Testament texts and signifying their fulfillment in this messy, cantankerous church in Corinth (and other churches), all rooted and made most demonstrable in the descent of the Holy Spirit. The Old Testament anticipated a day when God would establish a "new covenant" (Jer. 31:31; cf. 2 Cor. 3:6) with his people, promising, "I will put my law within them, and I will write it on their hearts" (Jer. 31:33; cf. 2 Cor. 3:2–3). This widespread internalization of God's redemptive work is even clearer in Ezekiel, where God promised his people, "I will give you a new heart, and a new *spirit* I will put within you" (Ezek. 36:26); he would "remove the heart of stone . . . and give them a heart of flesh" (Ezek. 11:19; cf. 2 Cor. 3:2–3).[12] The tablets of stone on which the Ten Commandments were etched would be replaced as the Spirit himself wrote on the hearts of God's people. God had always indicated internal transformation was needed (Deut. 10:16; Prov. 7:3; Jer. 4:4), and even from early times he also indicated that he would have to take matters into his own hands to execute this (Deut. 30:6). Now, after centuries of failure on the part of his people, he is mercifully doing so. He is no

---

10 The next few paragraphs are adapted from my commentary, Dane Ortlund, *2 Corinthians*, in *Romans–Galatians*, vol. 10 of *ESV Expository Commentary* (Wheaton, IL: Crossway, 2020), 437–40. Used by permission.

11 This redemptive-historical focus is a particular emphasis in Ridderbos, *Paul*, 218–23.

12 Note the ESV textual note in 3:3 at "human hearts," which literally reads "fleshly hearts," picking up the language of "heart of flesh" in Ezek. 11:19 and 36:26 (the Greek of 2 Cor. 3:3 and the Greek of Ezek. 36:26 and 11:19 in the Septuagint match exactly).

longer commanding them from the outside; he is transforming them from the inside. This is the glory and wonder of life in the new realm. Paul will continue to draw on these whole-Bible categories as he moves into 2 Corinthians 3:3–6.

Paul returns to the eschatological significance of the Holy Spirit in 3:6. Continuing the sentence begun in 3:5, Paul drills in more deeply to this God-given sufficiency. Paul has said *that* his sufficiency is from God in 3:5; now he explains *why*—that is, to what purpose. God has, to render the text woodenly, "sufficiented us" as ministers of a new covenant, the new and final day when God himself would decisively take matters into his own hands and place his Spirit within his people. God has not simply rendered Paul and his co-laborers sufficient for ministry in a general way. More specifically, God has established them as heralds of the long-awaited latter days in which the Messiah would come, the Spirit would be poured out, and the people of God would be restored. They are stewards and proclaimers of the "new covenant"—a time foretold in the Old Testament in which all God's promises reach their zenith. (Remember that Paul has already claimed that "all the promises of God" find fulfillment in Christ in 1:20, discussed above.) Paul will speak of the "new creation" in 5:17, though there the Spirit is not explicitly mentioned. Here Paul refers to a "new covenant," with the Spirit as the key element. In the coming of the Spirit on all God's people, what was expected to erupt at the end of history has erupted in the middle of history.

Paul explains the new covenant ministry as being "not of the letter but of the Spirit." And why? "For the letter[13] kills, but the Spirit gives life" (3:6). Returning to the Spirit (cf. 3:3), the supreme sign that the eschaton has dawned, Paul sets letter and Spirit over against each other as distinct aeons in redemptive history, the latter having eclipsed the former in the coming of Christ and the descent of the Spirit. "Letter" stands in for the entire ministry age of Moses and what Paul will call in 3:14 "the old covenant" in contrast to the new (cf. Heb. 8:6, 13). Paul has just spoken

---

13 "Letter" in 3:6 (*gramma*) refers to letters of the alphabet and should not be confused with "letter" in 3:3 (*epistolē*), which refers to epistles.

in 3:3 of "tablets of stone" as a way of referring to the Old Testament law and especially the Ten Commandments, so "letter" in 3:6 is likely a gloss for the way in which God's workings with his people in the Old Testament were mediated through a written code (cf. Rom. 2:25–29; 7:6). What then is the basic difference between the letter and the Spirit? The letter is outside in; the Spirit is inside out. Consequently, "The letter kills, but the Spirit gives life" (2 Cor. 3:6). One Greek verb (*zōopoieō*) renders "gives life"; it means "makes alive." This is resurrection language. The letter can only kill, because God's command plus the human heart left to its own devices yields only death and condemnation. The letter bounces off of hard human hearts, deflected, impotent. But what if God himself were to get inside the human heart, soften it, melt it—in short, make alive? What if God were to bring life where only death reigned? This ancient hope is what Paul is claiming to have transpired in his ministry to the Corinthians (also reflected in his argument in Romans at Rom. 7:6). One scholar justifiably calls 2 Corinthians 3:6 "stunningly bold."[14] The end-time resurrection long anticipated by God's people has broken in on this death-dominated world. Those in Christ are "made alive" by the Spirit now, and this spiritual resurrection will one day receive its inevitable consummation, physical and invincible resurrection.

We see a fourth and final reference to the Spirit in 2 Corinthians 3: "Now if the ministry of death, carved in letters on stone, came with such glory that the Israelites could not gaze at Moses' face because of its glory, which was being brought to an end, will not the ministry of the Spirit have even more glory?" (2 Cor. 3:7–8). The "ministry of death" is contrasted with the "ministry of the Spirit," encouraging us to understand the Spirit in terms of resurrection life—precisely what Paul has already made explicit in 3:6 in speaking of the life-giving Spirit and that he develops at greater length in Romans 7–8. Romans 8:10–11 is particularly illuminating in understanding the connection between the Spirit and resurrection life:

14 Dennis E. Johnson, "The Holy Spirit: New-Creation Power for God's Redeemed People," in *Theology for Ministry: How Doctrine Affects Pastoral Life and Practice*, ed. W. R. Edwards, J. C. Ferguson, and C. V. Dixhoorn (Phillipsburg, NJ: P&R, 2022), 197.

> If Christ is in you, although the body is dead because of sin, the Spirit is life because of righteousness. If the Spirit of him who raised Jesus from the dead dwells in you, he who raised Christ Jesus from the dead will also give life to your mortal bodies through his Spirit who dwells in you. (Rom. 8:10–11)

The Spirit raised Christ; that same Spirit is in us believers; the Spirit will raise us.

In the theology of the apostle Paul, the descent and democratization of the Spirit into and throughout God's people signals the dawning new creation and initiates the life of the age to come. Even in this new realm our physical bodies still run down and perish, for the old age remains. But it is even more deeply and wonderfully real that those united to Christ and thus indwelt by the Spirit are guaranteed final resurrection life. Indeed, this life has already begun (2 Cor. 4:7–11; cf. Eph. 2:5–6; Col. 3:1). In 2 Corinthians 3:8 Paul thus brings together the closely associated notions of the Spirit, resurrection, and glory in speaking of the dawning new age.

Other Uses of Spirit Language in 2 Corinthians

We now turn, thirdly and more briefly, to a few other places in 2 Corinthians where the Spirit is mentioned. How do these texts fill out our understanding of the Spirit that we have seen in the previous two sections?

It's important to notice that the Greek word *pneuma* is not always a reference to the Holy Spirit, the third person in the Trinity. Sometimes *pneuma* clearly refers to a human's "spirit" (2:13; 7:1, 13), and other times it is difficult to know whether Paul refers to the human spirit or the Holy Spirit—or perhaps some combination of both (4:13; 12:18).[15]

---

15 It is worth noting in passing the frequent use in Paul's letters of the adjective *pneumatikos*. The vast majority of New Testament instances of this word should almost certainly be capitalized; when Paul speaks of that which is *pneumatikos*, he is referring to that which is associated with the Spirit, not that which is immaterial or some other connotation readers of English may have with our term "spiritual."

In three further texts in 2 Corinthians, however, we do see Paul referring to the Holy Spirit: 3:17–18; 6:6; 11:4.

In 3:17–18, first, Paul says, "Now the Lord is the Spirit, and where the Spirit of the Lord is, there is freedom. And we all, with unveiled face, beholding the glory of the Lord, are being transformed into the same image from one degree of glory to another. For this comes from the Lord who is the Spirit." We have already considered this text above in looking at inaugurated eschatology generally in 2 Corinthians, and here we zero in only on the Spirit in the text, who is mentioned three times in short compass. In chapter 1, I suggested that "from glory to glory" (*apo doxēs eis doxan* in 3:18) means "from the glory of the old realm to the glory of the new realm." Here I add the observation that this transition from old-age glory to new-age glory is deeply and explicitly *aligned with the ministry of the Spirit*: "this comes from the Lord who is the Spirit." Indeed, the ESV text breaks into two sentences what in Greek is one sentence. To put 3:18 more transparently, we "are being transformed into the same image from glory to glory, as from the Lord, the Spirit."[16] A further theological observation is the intimately close association—not confusion, but close identification—of the Lord (Jesus) with "the Spirit." We see Paul maintaining his Trinitarianism within a retained monotheism.

Second, moving to 2 Corinthians 6, the first ten verses of this chapter are one sentence in Greek, part of which reads as follows, as Paul describes what ministry leadership looks like in the new realm:

> as servants of God we commend ourselves in every way: by great endurance, in afflictions, hardships, calamities, beatings, imprisonments, riots, labors, sleepless nights, hunger; by purity, knowledge, patience, kindness, the Holy Spirit, genuine love; by truthful speech, and the power of God; with the weapons of righteousness for the right hand and for the left. (2 Cor. 6:4–7)

---

16 For further on this, see Dane C. Ortlund, "'From Glory to Glory': 2 Corinthians 3:18 in Biblical-Theological Perspective," *CTJ* 54, no. 1 (2019): 22–23.

Both here and in 2 Corinthians 11, Paul describes his ministry experiences by bringing together two ends of the spectrum—both glory and pain, both outer discomfort and also inner marks of the new realm. In 6:6 Paul mentions "the Holy Spirit." At this juncture all I wish to point out is the seamless way in which Paul integrates the Spirit into the other marks of the "day of salvation" that has dawned in Jesus Christ. That is, in 6:2 Paul claims that the longed-for day of salvation of which Isaiah prophesied (Isa. 49:8 // 2 Cor. 6:2) had arrived in the first century, *and one mark of that dawning new day is the arrival of the Spirit.*

Third and finally, in 11:4 Paul correlates three realities:

1. the "Jesus . . . we proclaimed";
2. the "s/Spirit . . . you received";
3. the "gospel . . . you accepted."

Not much need be said except to note the tightly bound triad of Jesus, Spirit, and gospel, all of which belong to the new realm—Jesus and gospel, to be sure, and along with them the Spirit.

One final line of thought is worth mentioning with regard to the Spirit in 2 Corinthians as the chief marker of the dawning new realm in Paul's ministry and in time. In exploring various texts in chapter 1 of the present volume that reflect inaugurated eschatology in 2 Corinthians, we looked at 6:16, which makes an overt claim that God's people in this time between Christ's two comings "are the temple of the living God." This temple theme itself links with the Spirit, both reflecting the long-awaited eschaton. This is because in Acts 2, when the Spirit falls on God's people, *the way this descent is framed is as the coming final temple.* To pursue this claim would take us beyond the bounds of 2 Corinthians, so we must curtail the otherwise enjoyable exploration of Acts 2 this would involve. I instead point readers to G. K. Beale's two-part exploration of this point.[17] In passing we should

---

17   G. K. Beale, "The Descent of the Eschatological Temple in the Form of the Spirit at Pentecost: Part I," *TynBul* 56, no. 1 (2005): 73–102; G. K. Beale, "The Descent of the Eschatological Temple in the Form of the Spirit at Pentecost: Part II," *TynBul* 56, no. 2 (2005): 63–90.

see an organic connection between the Spirit (esp. 1:22; 5:5) and the temple (esp. 6:16) in 2 Corinthians, working in tandem to present the church as the latter-day people of God.

Synthesis of Paul's Theology of the Spirit in 2 Corinthians

Let us draw together in brief summary what we have seen in this chapter. Four points merit mentioning.

First, the Spirit is the mark that the new realm has dawned. As Vos states,

> It is the Spirit of God who gives form and character to the eschatological life in the broadest and most pervasive sense, that the coming age is the age of the Spirit *par excellence*, so that all that enters into it, forms part of it, or takes place in it, must necessarily be baptized into the Pneuma as into an omnipresent reality and thus itself become "spiritual" in its mode of existence and quality.[18]

Jesus Christ launched the new realm but then physically relocated back up to heaven. The abiding mark of the new realm is his own Spirit, living in his people, constituting the new and final temple and fulfilling the prophetic hope of the pouring out of God's Spirit.

Second, there is no going backward once one has the Spirit—no "hitting rewind." As the *arrabōn*, the Spirit is the "down payment" who thus guarantees eventual final salvation, bodily resurrection, and life in the new earth.

Third, the Spirit is inseparably associated with resurrection life. This is the significance of the opening verses of 2 Corinthians 3, where we read that the result of "the letter" (the Mosaic code, left to our own self-resourced attempts at fulfillment) is death, whereas the end result of the Spirit is life (3:6). By "life" is meant the resurrection life of the new realm. Just as Christ's crucifixion and resurrection each synecdochically imply the other when only one is mentioned, so also with

---

18 Vos, "The Eschatological Aspect," 122.

the Spirit and resurrection life: to mention one, in Paul's writings, is to necessarily imply the other.

Fourth, the Spirit is the inaugural experience of the new realm. To enjoy the presence of the Spirit is to enjoy, here and now, the life of the age to come. The old age still presses in on us from every direction and even remains within each believer. Remnants of the old realm cling to us. But believers have already begun to taste the life of the new realm as they enjoy a life animated by the very Spirit of God within them. Even though 2 Corinthians does not emphasize the experiential aspect of the Spirit but rather focuses on the Spirit as the mark of the dawning new realm, we ought to remember the experiential side that Paul teaches in Romans and Galatians when those letters speak of the Spirit causing our own hearts to leap up and cry "Abba, Father!" (Rom. 8:15; Gal. 4:6). What does this Spiritual life look like? Though Paul does not use the phrase "fruit of the Spirit" in 2 Corinthians as he does in Galatians, we could view 2 Corinthians 6:3–10 as the Corinthian parallel to Galatians 5:22–23, where Paul does use the phrase "fruit of the Spirit." The Spiritual life of the new realm looks like "purity, knowledge, patience, kindness, the Holy Spirit, genuine love" (2 Cor. 6:6).

In a word: The Spirit is the mark of the new realm, the guarantee of the new realm, the agent of resurrection life of the new realm, and the experience of the new realm.

4

Satan

The Enemy of New Realm Ministry

WHETHER FROM EMBARRASSMENT, fear, or ignorance, we do not tend to speak much of Satan in the church today. But he is the savage enemy and accuser of God's people according to the consistent testimony of Scripture, Old Testament and New. In 2 Corinthians we come upon some particularly illuminating comments from Paul on Satan, meriting a chapter of its own to consider the contribution of 2 Corinthians to a Christian understanding of Satan. It is fitting for this chapter on the saints' great invisible enemy to follow the chapter on the Spirit, the saints' great invisible ally.

Paul assumes his readers are aware of Satan. In none of his letters does he seek to explain the reality of Satan to his churches as a hitherto unknown reality. Rather, he more passingly mentions the person and activity of Satan. As he does so, we are fortified with crucial insight into the battle that Christians are waging with the invisible but real forces of hell.

Paul mentions Satan in six texts in 2 Corinthians (2:11; 4:4; 6:15; 11:3, 14; 12:7), more than any other Pauline letter. Three times we find *ho satana* ("Satan" or "the Satan," 2:11; 11:14; 12:7). The other three titles each occur once: *ho theos tou aiōnos toutou* ("the god of this age," 4:4), *Beliar* ("Beliar" or "Belial," 6:15), and *ho ophis* ("the serpent," 11:3).

The occurrences are spread fairly evenly throughout the letter, making it easy to overlook how pervasive a theme it is. When one stops and takes notice of all of them together, however, the prominence of Satan in 2 Corinthians emerges with striking clarity. Although each one is only a passing reference, the cumulative effect is a fairly comprehensive understanding of Paul's theology of Satan. We will take them each in turn.

2 Corinthians 2:11 (in the Context of 2:5–11)

Now if anyone has caused pain, he has caused it not to me, but in some measure—not to put it too severely—to all of you. For such a one, this punishment by the majority is enough, so you should rather turn to forgive and comfort him, or he may be overwhelmed by excessive sorrow. So I beg you to reaffirm your love for him. For this is why I wrote, that I might test you and know whether you are obedient in everything. Anyone whom you forgive, I also forgive. Indeed, what I have forgiven, if I have forgiven anything, has been for your sake in the presence of Christ, so that we would not be outwitted by Satan; for we are not ignorant of his designs. (2 Cor. 2:5–11)

In this first occurrence we see Paul refer to Satan's strategy of exploitation. The immediate context here is a matter of forgiveness, as Paul communicates his solidarity with the Corinthians as they freshly enter into Christian fellowship with this brother. The apostle is exhorting the Corinthians to re-embrace the offending but now penitent brother. The juxtaposition Paul then establishes as he closes this exhortation is striking indeed: if the Corinthians fail to forgive this brother, they are being "outwitted" by Satan himself. The verb for "outwitted" (*pleonekteō*) occurs just five times in the New Testament, four of them in 2 Corinthians (2:11; 7:2; 12:17, 18; 1 Thess. 4:6). The other three uses in 2 Corinthians are translated by the ESV as "taken advantage of" and are Paul's insistence that he and his partners have not taken advantage of the Corinthians, presumably referring to a charge the super-apostles are making of Paul in his absence.

Mindful of the other uses of this verb, in conjunction with the immediate context of 2:5–11, the idea Paul seems to be attributing to Satan is one of deceiving *exploitation*. If the Corinthians withhold forgiveness, continuing to hold this penitent brother at arm's length because of his offense, Satan is tactically outmaneuvering them. To Paul, continued judging of a penitent brother is to unwittingly link arms with Satan, while extending forgiveness is a tactical defeat of Satan.

2 Corinthians 4:4 (in the Context of 4:1–4)

Therefore, having this ministry by the mercy of God, we do not lose heart. But we have renounced disgraceful, underhanded ways. We refuse to practice cunning or to tamper with God's word, but by the open statement of the truth we would commend ourselves to everyone's conscience in the sight of God. And even if our gospel is veiled, it is veiled to those who are perishing. In their case the god of this world has blinded the minds of the unbelievers, to keep them from seeing the light of the gospel of the glory of Christ, who is the image of God. (2 Cor. 4:1–4)

This is a particularly instructive reference to Satan. But is the phrase "the god of this age"[1] a reference to Satan in the first place? While we should not be overly dogmatic, the evidence does strongly suggest so. First, we have already drawn attention to the repeated references to Satan in a number of ways throughout 2 Corinthians. Second, here in our immediate context Paul sets the god of this age opposite Christ and speaks of him as blinding unbelievers spiritually, which is consistent with the broader biblical reality of Satan as a deceiver. Third, Paul uses a similar phrase in Ephesians 2:2 when he refers to "the prince of the power of the air," and the two texts are probably mutually illuminating, referring to the real but transient power Satan presently wields.

---

1   For reasons given in chapter 2 (see p. 47), I will render this text "god of the age" and not "god of this world" throughout the rest of the present volume.

Of particular interest to the present study is the eschatological significance of this reference to Satan. By calling Satan "the god of this
age," Paul brings us into the two-age macro-historical schema of early
Judaism and Christianity, discussed above. The old realm is the present
age, while the new realm is the age to come, which has broken into,
overlays, and replaces the present age as believers' fundamental place of
belonging. And the old realm is, so to speak, the arena of Satanic rule.
This is not to say that God does not rule over all that happens with regard to both ages. Rather, subsumed within God's exhaustive sovereign
will (e.g., Eph. 1:11) is the powerful influence of Satan with the present
age and all that goes along with it—sin, death, condemnation, and so
on. In referring to Satan as "the god of this age," we could reasonably
surmise that, though Paul never puts it this explicitly, he views Jesus
as "the ruler of the age to come." Each realm has its respective ruler.
The two are not equal and opposite powers of course. But each is the
dominant presiding influence of the two respective ages.

2 Corinthians 6:15 (in the Context of 6:14–16a)

> Do not be unequally yoked with unbelievers. For what partnership
> has righteousness with lawlessness? Or what fellowship has light
> with darkness? What accord has Christ with Belial? Or what portion
> does a believer share with an unbeliever? What agreement has the
> temple of God with idols? For we are the temple of the living God.
> (2 Cor. 6:14–16a)

The unusual word "Belial" (Greek *Beliar*) refers to Satan, as evidenced in Second Temple Jewish literature (e.g., Testament of Levi
18:12) and transliterates a Hebrew term denoting "worthlessness" or
"destruction."[2] Throughout this section of his letter (6:14–7:1), Paul
is bringing out the mutually exclusive nature of the old realm with
the new. Though the two are presently coexisting, they cannot mix or

---

2   See the useful discussion of Murray J. Harris, *The Second Epistle to the Corinthians*, NIGTC
    (Grand Rapids, MI: Eerdmans, 2005), 502–3.

blend, and believers in Christ must live accordingly. Righteousness and lawlessness (6:14), light and darkness (6:14), Christ and Belial (6:15)— each pair contains polar opposites, inherently opposed to each other. Paul has just proclaimed that the Corinthians live in the longed-for day of salvation of which Isaiah prophesied (6:2). He is about to claim that believers are the latter-day temple of God (6:16). And in between these two towering claims he mentions Satan and the absolute antithesis between him and Christ—which is roughly to say, between his *realm* and Christ's.

2 Corinthians 11:3 (in the Context of 11:1–5)

I wish you would bear with me in a little foolishness. Do bear with me! For I feel a divine jealousy for you, since I betrothed you to one husband, to present you as a pure virgin to Christ. But I am afraid that as the serpent deceived Eve by his cunning, your thoughts will be led astray from a sincere and pure devotion to Christ. For if someone comes and proclaims another Jesus than the one we proclaimed, or if you receive a different spirit from the one you received, or if you accept a different gospel from the one you accepted, you put up with it readily enough. Indeed, I consider that I am not in the least inferior to these super-apostles. (2 Cor. 11:1–5)

Paul is picking up the whole-Bible theme of marital-jealousy-as-spiritual-metaphor.[3] Normally the referents are God and his people, though here Paul casts himself as feeling jealous for the Corinthians on behalf of Christ, the husband to whom they have been betrothed. In 11:3 Paul expresses his fear that the Corinthians will be lured away "from a sincere and pure devotion" to Christ. Presumably the "someone" who "comes and proclaims another Jesus than the one we proclaimed" (11:4) refers to the super-apostles since Paul goes on in the next verse to claim no inferiority "to these super-apostles" (11:5).

3 See Raymond C. Ortlund, *God's Unfaithful Wife: A Biblical Theology of Spiritual Adultery*, NSBT 2 (Downers Grove, IL: InterVarsity Press, 2003).

What concerns us at the moment is the first half of 11:3 where Paul slips in an ancient account to drive home his point: "I am afraid that as the serpent deceived Eve by his cunning, your thoughts will be led astray." "Serpent" is the longest-tenured way of speaking of Satan in the Bible, reaching all the way back to Genesis 3 (the only other Pauline use of the term is 1 Cor. 10:9, referring to the serpents of Num. 21).[4] Paul is viewing the Corinthians in the position of Eve and viewing the super-apostles in the position of the serpent, Satan. The particular activity of Satan that Paul names is "deceiving," and the weapon used for such deception is "cunning" (used five times in the New Testament, including at 2 Cor. 4:2 where Paul denies walking in "cunning," earlier in the verse described as "disgraceful" and "underhanded").

Slippery subterfuge is Satan's natural language and regular *modus operandi* as he seeks to confound and destroy God's people.

2 Corinthians 11:14 (in the Context of 11:12–15)

And what I am doing I will continue to do, in order to undermine the claim of those who would like to claim that in their boasted mission they work on the same terms as we do. For such men are false apostles, deceitful workmen, disguising themselves as apostles of Christ. And no wonder, for even Satan disguises himself as an angel of light. So it is no surprise if his servants, also, disguise themselves as servants of righteousness. Their end will correspond to their deeds. (2 Cor. 11:12–15)

Shortly after referencing the deceiving work of Satan in Genesis 3 and associating it with the cunning deceitfulness of the super-apostles (11:4–5), Paul once more aligns Satan and the super-apostles with a fascinating insight into how Satan operates. In his most castigating remark about the super-apostles, Paul calls them "false apostles, deceitful workmen, disguising themselves as apostles of Christ" (11:13). He then makes the connection: "And no wonder, for even Satan disguises

---

4   See Andrew D. Naselli, *The Serpent and the Serpent Slayer*, SSBT (Wheaton, IL: Crossway, 2020).

himself as an angel of light" (11:14). Paul's reference to "light" here perhaps hearkens back to 2 Corinthians 6, where he spoke of the opposition of light and darkness immediately prior to the opposition of Christ and Beliar. (Both passages also have "righteousness" language: 6:14; 11:15.)

The unique light that is shed in this passage on Paul's theology of Satan is in saying he "disguises himself as an angel of light." The only two places outside of this passage where Paul uses this word for "disguise" (*metaschēmatizō*) are 1 Corinthians 4:6 ("I have *applied* all these things to myself and Apollos") and Philippians 3:21 (Christ "will *transform* our lowly body to be like his glorious body"). The first of these is minimally illuminating; the second of somewhat more interest. Most instructive will simply be to note the immediate context and usage in 2 Corinthians 11. Paul has reiterated the notion of deception in calling the super-apostles "deceitful workmen" in 11:13. This notion of deception is ratcheted up as Paul then says Satan disguises himself by transforming into an angel of light. Satan is a master craftsman in disguise and deceit, cloaking himself as beauty and goodness. He lures people away from light by pretending to be light himself.

2 Corinthians 12:7 (in the Context of 12:7–10)

So to keep me from becoming conceited because of the surpassing greatness of the revelations, a thorn was given me in the flesh, a messenger of Satan to harass me, to keep me from becoming conceited. Three times I pleaded with the Lord about this, that it should leave me. But he said to me, "My grace is sufficient for you, for my power is made perfect in weakness." Therefore I will boast all the more gladly of my weaknesses, so that the power of Christ may rest upon me. For the sake of Christ, then, I am content with weaknesses, insults, hardships, persecutions, and calamities. For when I am weak, then I am strong. (2 Cor. 12:7–10)

The final and most famous reference to Satan comes in 2 Corinthians 12. The immediate action ascribed to Satan is, according to the

ESV, that of harassment (12:7), though the verb used (*kolaphizō*) and its other four New Testament occurrences (including Christ's treatment on trial at the hands of the Jewish authorities) refer to physical abuse (Matt. 26:67; Mark 14:65; 1 Cor. 4:11; 1 Pet. 2:20). We cannot confidently assert whether Paul is referring to Satan indirectly abusing him physically through the hands of humans or to a more spiritual and direct sort of harassment or abuse. Paul does describe the same affliction in the immediately preceding phrase as "a thorn in the *flesh*," but he commonly uses the term "flesh" to refer to immaterial reality, and in any event the entire phrase "thorn in the flesh" could easily be a metaphor for some nonphysical trial. Scholars and pastors continue to speculate as to the precise nature of this trial, but the more immediate point of Paul's statement is not the content of the thorn but its intent—namely, Paul's own humility.

That humbling intent of the thorn brings us to the immediate takeaway for our purposes as we consider Paul's theology of Satan in 2 Corinthians. The conclusion is inescapable that Satan is attacking Paul under the divine oversight and even providential directing of God. I stake this assertion not on the likely divine passive "was given" but on the broader point that the purpose of the thorn is Paul's humility. Satan would not have had Paul's sanctification and humility as a goal. That is God's desire, not Satan's. Yet the purpose of the thorn, as Paul states twice in short compass at both the beginning and the end of 12:7, was "to keep me from becoming conceited." Some translations omit the repetition (e.g., NIV, CEV), but this blunts the literary force of the double claim.

The theological takeaway of this passage with regard to Satan takes us deep into the mysterious workings of the sovereign care of God for his people. We ought not explain away what baffles human mental capacities if we see it in Scripture; both here and throughout Scripture we find God's comprehensive sovereignty and Satan's malicious activity overlaid. One does not begin where the other ends; rather, Satan's activity is entirely subsumed within the sovereign will of God. I have heard preachers say Satan is "on a leash," but that does not quite capture the point accurately, for it communicates that Satan does whatever he wants up to a certain point and does so against the will of the leash-holder. No, God's work and Satan's are overlaid, yet in such a way that God himself does not and cannot commit evil (James 1:13–17).

Theologians and philosophers have long wrestled with this "antinomy"[5] of God's "decretive will" by which he ordains all things and his "preceptive will" by which he desires only some things.[6] I will not seek to resolve this but rather allow to stand both scriptural truths of Satanic power and the wraparound of divine sovereignty. I recognize that this may be hard for some readers to accept, so let me mention one other passage, this time from the Old Testament, to make the same point. In Job's sufferings we are twice told of God's mysterious, non-morally culpable ruling of Satan's afflicting of Job. When his children die, Job says, "The LORD gave, and the LORD has taken away; blessed be the name of the LORD" (Job 1:21), and we are immediately given the inspired commentary: "In all this Job did not sin or charge God with wrong" (Job 1:22). And in the next chapter when Job's own body is afflicted, Job responds to his wife's challenge to curse God: "Shall we receive good from God, and shall we not receive evil?" (Job 2:10). And once again we have commentary endorsing Job's theology: "In all this Job did not sin with his lips" (Job 2:10). As with Paul in the New Testament, Job in the Old Testament suffered severe anguish at the immediate hand of Satan yet, at the same time, anguish that was under the sovereign will of God.

Conclusion

Of particular interest given the thrust of the present volume is the way in which Paul speaks of Satan in an eschatologically informed way in at

---

5   This is the word J. I. Packer uses to describe the relationship between divine sovereignty and human responsibility in his classic study *Evangelism and the Sovereignty of God* (Leicester, UK: Inter-Varsity Press, 1961).

6   The most biblically grounded and philosophically reasoned study of the two wills in God that I have come across is that of Jonathan Edwards, which he wrestled with in what he called his "Miscellanies" (private theological reflections) in *The "Miscellanies," Entry Nos a–z, aa–zz, 1–500*, ed. Thomas A. Schafer, vol. 13 of *The Works of Jonathan Edwards* (New Haven, CT: Yale University Press, 1994), as well as in his *Freedom of the Will*, ed. Paul Ramsey, vol. 1 of *The Works of Jonathan Edwards* (New Haven, CT: Yale University Press, 1957).

least two of these texts (2 Cor. 4:1–4; 6:14–16). I do not mean to communicate that Satan only arrived on the scene in the New Testament and the dawn of the new realm. It is reasonable to surmise, however, that just as the Spirit was active in the Old Testament but flooded out more deeply and widely in the New, so too Satan was active in the Old Testament but has accelerated his activity in the new realm. His malice has intensified, as he knows that God's sprouting new realm has decisively undermined his rule as "the god of this age."

In short, then, in 2 Corinthians we have seen Satan as the great exploiter of God's people, tactically seeking to prevent forgiveness of one another (2:5–11), as the god of this present age in contrast to the age to come, operating as a powerful influence that is antithetical to the new realm that Christ and the Spirit brought (4:1–4), as the "worthlessness" that is the photo negative of the aeonic day of salvation of which the Old Testament prophesied (6:14–16), as the ancient deceiver of God's people (11:1–5), as the master manipulator and pretender who feigns holiness and beauty (11:12–15), and as the one who, for all his cruel intent, operates according to the all-encompassing rule of God (12:7–10).

5

Friendship

The Method of New Realm Ministry

ON INITIAL REFLECTION it may seem a bit of a stretch to include a chapter on friendship in a theology of one of Paul's letters. Indeed, standard Pauline theologies contain little or no reflection on the significance of friendship to Paul's thinking.[1] The possible objections are twofold. First, is friendship a properly theological matter in the first place? Second, even if friendship is a theological matter generally speaking, does Paul's theology reflect any particular focus on friendship?

The two objections, and their answers, are intertwined with one another. In what follows I would like to explore the evidence in 2 Corinthians for how Paul thought about Christian fellowship and friendship, and in the course of doing so we will handle both objections together.

A word on definitions. I am using *friendship* in this chapter quite broadly to speak of healthy Christian fellowship. The reason I am not mainly using a word such as *fellowship* or *community* is that these blander terms lack the connotation of collegial camaraderie and

---

1 Though not part of a comprehensive Pauline theology, a notable exception to the neglect is David E. Briones, "Why Can't We Be Friends? Paul and Aristotle on Friendship," in *Paul and the Giants of Philosophy: Reading the Apostle in Greco-Roman Context*, ed. Joseph R. Dodson and David E. Briones (Downers Grove, IL: IVP Academic, 2019), 36–49, which focuses on differences and similarities between Paul's notion of friendship and Aristotle's—with recourse particularly to Philippians.

affection that *friendship* invokes. For Paul, his heart was bound up with his teammates and partners in ministry. The extended section on financial giving (2 Cor. 8–9) will accordingly be subsumed within this broader reflection on friendship in 2 Corinthians.

Paul and Friendship in the Broader New Testament

Before moving to 2 Corinthians, it will be useful to note briefly the broader evidence in the New Testament that Christian friendship mattered deeply to Paul. Only a facile reading of the New Testament would support the notion that Paul was a solitary and isolated leader, thinking and traveling on his own, stiff-arming the friends that less spiritually mature Christians (so to speak) might need. On the contrary, in Acts we see Paul traveling with companions as his standard operating procedure (e.g., Acts 13:1–3, 13; 14:1; 15:2; 32, 40; 16:3; 17:10; 18:2–3; 19:29). One particularly beautiful episode in Acts is when Paul wished to engage a riotous crowd in Ephesus but "some of the Asiarchs, *who were friends of his*, sent to him and were urging him not to venture into the theater" (Acts 19:31). And throughout his letters we see evidence of the significance of friendship for Paul in at least three ways.

First, in only five of his thirteen letters does Paul identify himself as the sole source of the letter, and three of those five (1–2 Timothy and Titus) are written to a single individual, so it would make sense that Paul make each a one-to-one correspondence. His standard operating procedure was to signal his non-solitary ministry right from the start of his letters.

Second, even when Paul does not identify teammates at his side in his opening greeting (e.g., Romans and Ephesians), he invariably closes with a sign-off that explicitly loops in ministry colleagues and friends, sometimes at great length (Rom. 16:1–24, esp. 16:21–23; Eph. 6:21–23).

Third, we see particularly heartful expressions from Paul reflecting longing and interpersonal pathos in the bodies of his letters. We think of Paul's affectionate recalling of Timothy's tears when they were together and his longing to see him (2 Tim. 1:4), his repeated plea that Timothy come to him as soon as possible (2 Tim. 4:9, 21), and the apparently restored confidence in Mark (2 Tim. 4:11) after the "sharp disagreement" with Barnabas over Mark in Acts 15:39—a disagreement that did not send Paul into isolation but rather moved him to bring a different ministry partner, Silas. Consider also the deep affection Paul expresses toward the Thessalonians, describing his feelings for them in both maternal and paternal terms (1 Thess. 2:7, 11). We think of the single most famous expression of justification by faith in all the Bible (Gal. 2:16) and recognize that it comes in the pursuit of restored table fellowship among Christians (Gal. 2:11–21). And of course the sole purpose of the brief letter of Philemon is horizontal reconciliation.

As I focus on the corporate reality of friendship and fellowship in Paul's ministry generally and in 2 Corinthians specifically, we must not lose sight of the irreducible role the individual plays in Paul's understanding of life in Christ. Some strands of recent and current Pauline studies so emphasize the corporate dimensions to Paul's thought— an emphasis that surely has been needed—that the individual recedes overly much into the background.[2] We must maintain in our study of Paul a balanced vision of both the need for every individual to yield to Christ in faith, repentance, mortification of sin, keeping in step with the Spirit, and all the rest while also maintaining a deep awareness of the body into which each individual Christian has been incorporated and without which each individual Christian will wither and languish.[3]

Paul and Friendship in 2 Corinthians

"Paul had a few precious friends, and he did not mind admitting so"[4]— indeed, more than a few, as we take stock of 2 Corinthians! Against this

---

2   E.g., Krister Stendahl, "The Apostle Paul and the Introspective Conscience of the West," *HTR* 56, no. 3 (1963): 199–215; Timothy G. Gombis, *The Drama of Ephesians: Participating in the Triumph of God* (Downers Grove, IL: IVP Academic, 2010).

3   The individual is helpfully emphasized in Gary W. Burnett, *Paul and the Salvation of the Individual*, Biblical Interpretation 57 (Leiden: Brill, 2001). See the judicious balancing of corporate and individual in Douglas J. Moo, *A Theology of Paul and His Letters: The Gift of the New Realm in Christ*, BTNT (Grand Rapids, MI: Zondervan Academic, 2021), 31–35, 568–69. See also B. C. Dunson, *Individual and Community in Paul's Letter to the Romans*, WUNT 2/332 (Tübingen: Mohr Siebeck, 2012).

4   William Edgar, "Afterword: Theological Reflections on the True Nature of Friendship," in *Theology for Ministry: How Doctrine Affects Pastoral Life and Practice*, ed. W. R. Edwards,

broader background above, what do we find when we come to 2 Corinthians specifically? In brief, we find Paul not only being consistent in terms of broader patterns but penning a letter that reflects perhaps the most robust theology of friendship in the New Testament (Philippians and Philemon being the two arguable rivals).

To be sure, we have the characteristic opening greeting (2 Cor. 1:1), which in this case includes Timothy in the letter's salutation (presumably an attribution of solidarity and ministry partnership, not coauthorship). And Paul closes by sending greetings from other believers (13:13).

But what is most striking in 2 Corinthians when it comes to friendship is the intimacy and relational pathos within the body of the letter itself. For all the theological profundity of the first chapter (sharing in Christ's sufferings, all three members of the Trinity mentioned in 1:3–21, etc.), Paul is not purely theologizing about matters between the individual Christian and God. Permeating this opening chapter is the first-person plural, not to mention the harrowing near-death experience of Paul and Timothy together. This leads into an expectation of mutual boasting—not, as in Galatians 6:14, boasting in the cross, but boasting in one another (2 Cor. 1:14; cf. 1 Thess. 2:19). Paul then goes into an extended defense of his delayed travel to be with the Corinthians (2 Cor. 1:15–24). All this testifies to the significance with which Paul took his relational life with other believers, and this is just the first chapter of the letter. As the letter goes on, we see that Paul did not simply value warm fellowship with other believers for its own sake, but he actually viewed believers in Christ as bound up with one another in a deep bond of spiritual solidarity as those jointly united to Christ.

The defense of his travel plans continues through 2:4, and then Paul launches into his exhortation to turn and embrace the penitent sinner (2:5–11). Not only do we have continued, sustained reflection from

---

J. C. A. Ferguson, and C. V. Dixhoorn (Phillipsburg, NJ: P&R, 2022), 555. Though the focus of this essay is not 2 Corinthians or even Paul, I commend the whole essay as a beautiful reflection on the nature of new realm friendship and the divine love that animates it, all consistent with the interpersonal realities permeating 2 Corinthians.

Paul on interpersonal realities at Corinth, but we note with special interest the way Paul opens this section: "Now if anyone has caused pain, he has caused it not to me, but in some measure—not to put it too severely—to all of you" (2:5). Paul is so bound up with the Corinthians that painful rejection of him reflects a concomitant painful rejection of the Corinthians. This is similar to what we read a few verses earlier when Paul says the same thing, though of joy rather than pain: "I felt sure of all of you, that my joy would be the joy of you all" (2:3).

Yes, Paul conceives of his relationship with his churches as teacher to pupil (1 Tim. 2:7), as builder to building (1 Cor. 3:9–10), as brother to brother and sister (pervasively throughout his letters), as coworkers in the gospel (1 Cor. 3:9), and even as father to children (1 Cor. 4:15). But most deeply he views his relationship with his churches as one of *Spiritual union and solidarity*.[5] Paul often wishes he could see his people face-to-face (Col. 2:1; 1 Thess. 2:17; 3:10). But whether he is near or far geographically, he is so deeply one with his people that as goes their fate so goes his. Both their joy and their grief are bound up with one another.

We see this continue throughout 2 Corinthians. While we cannot look at every example, two extended texts demand attention: chapter 7 and chapters 8–9.

Dying and Rising Together (2 Corinthians 7)

In chapter 7, Paul has just completed his discussion of Christians needing to categorically separate themselves from the defilements of the world—or to put it positively, to join themselves in close fellowship with believers. This flows naturally into a pivot from the Corinthians' relationships with other people to their relationship with Paul himself. Paul has exhorted them not to make room in their hearts for the world; now he asks that they *do* make room in their hearts for him (7:2)—or, more specifically, for Paul and his colleagues (note the continuing

---

5   I purposely capitalize the adjective to make explicit the working of the Holy Spirit in this union.

first-person plurals "us" and "we" throughout this section of the letter). What Paul says is without peer across the pages of the New Testament in terms of the depths of interpersonal order exposed:

> Make room in your hearts for us. We have wronged no one, we have corrupted no one, we have taken advantage of no one. I do not say this to condemn you, for I said before that you are in our hearts, to die together and to live together. I am acting with great boldness toward you; I have great pride in you; I am filled with comfort. In all our affliction, I am overflowing with joy. (7:2–4)

It takes little familiarity with Paul to pick up the emotional and relational intensity surfacing in these words. How much more will readers who are not only familiar with Paul but also well versed in Greek note the way his agitation even comes through in the terse and jagged syntax of the original text in these lines. For example, "Make room in your hearts for us" is actually the less elegant "Make room for us," just two words in Greek (*Chōrēsate hēmas*). Likewise the opening sentence of 7:3, to put it once more with maximal woodenness, reads, "For condemnation I do not speak" (*pros katakrisin ou legō*). If in the early chapters of Romans Paul is crafting an ornate and reasoned argument from his mind, in 2 Corinthians 7 it is as if Paul is blurting out visceral relational anguish from his heart. *Both* are holy Scripture. Indeed, both are *theological*. How so?

I will synthesize an answer to this question toward the end of this chapter, after we have looked at 2 Corinthians 8–9. For now, note the sublime claim Paul makes toward the end of 7:3: "You are in our hearts, to die together and to live together." What is so arresting in this phrase is the actual language Paul uses. For *he uses terms ordinarily employed when discussing the wondrous depths of union with Christ.* The verbs for "die together" (or "co-die," *synapothnēskō*) and "live together" (or "co-live," *synzaō*) cause Paul's notion of co-dying and co-rising with Christ himself to leap to mind. Paul has already in 2 Corinthians spoken in general terms of the death and resurrection life of Christ manifesting themselves in us who are united to him (4:10–12). Even more intriguing are the two other Pauline texts where Paul once again brings together the notion of "co-dying" and "co-rising" (no other New Testament writer uses these terms[6]). These are Romans 6:8 and 2 Timothy 2:11, included here with 2 Corinthians 7:3 for ease of reference:[7]

Now if we have died with Christ, we believe that we will also live with him [*ei de apethanomen syn Christō, pisteuomen hoti kai synzēsomen autō*]. (Rom. 6:8)

You are in our hearts, to die together and to live together [*en tais kardiais hēmōn este eis to synapothanein kai synzēn*]. (2 Cor. 7:3)

If we have died with him, we will also live with him [*ei gap synapethanomen, kai synzēsomen*]. (2 Tim. 2:11)

The text in Romans comes in the course of an extended reflection on union with Christ, with whom we have been united in both his death and resurrection (Rom. 6:1–11). It is probably the most systematic and searching teaching on union with Christ in the New Testament. In 2 Timothy 2:11, by contrast, much more briefly, Paul appears to be

---

6 We find the word *synapothnēskō* in Mark 14:31 as Peter pledges to be willing to die with Jesus. Nowhere else does *synzaō* occur in the New Testament, and nowhere but Rom. 6:8, 2 Cor. 7, and 2 Tim. 2:11 are the twin concepts of co-dying and co-rising brought together.

7 The text in 2 Timothy uses the same two verbs as 2 Cor. 7:3 (*synapothnēskō* and *synzaō*); Rom. 6:8 only uses *synzaō*, though the notion of co-dying with Christ is clearly in view with the phrase *apethanomen syn Christō*.

   Note: Greek grammars discuss the tendency for the letter *n* (Greek ν) to be either assimilated or not assimilated in words with the prefix *syn-* followed by a consonant, such as *synzaō*. This is reflected in New Testament manuscripts—some of which have *synzēn* and others *syzēn* at 2 Cor. 7:3 (so also in Rom. 6:8; 2 Tim. 2:11). Editors of published Greek New Testaments must decide which manuscript spelling to use. I have followed the spelling in *The Greek New Testament, Produced at Tyndale House, Cambridge*, ed. Dirk Jongkind (Wheaton, IL: Crossway, 2017), in which the *n* is not assimilated in the verb *synzaō*.

picking up some sort of preformed hymnic or creedal formula, the first line of which passingly mentions co-dying and co-rising with Christ. The point I wish to note is that we find ourselves with three texts in Paul's corpus in which he brings together solidarity in both dying and rising—a solidarity so intimate, so overlapping, that for one party to die or to live is for the party to whom they are united to experience the same death or life. We should not press this too far, nor should we box in the reality Paul is describing by overexplaining it. But clearly it would be difficult for Paul to describe a closer solidarity in this co-dying and co-rising. The other two Pauline instances of co-dying and co-rising are of the believer co-dying and co-rising with Christ; in 2 Corinthians 7:3 Paul applies the same categories to Christian fellowship. Paul flops on its side the wondrous truth of union with Christ in his death and resurrection and speaks in the same way of believers and the existence they share together in this new realm that Christ and the Spirit inaugurated.

The past few generations of Pauline scholarship have robustly emphasized the theme of union with Christ, both with general explorations of the subject[8] as well as specifically Pauline studies.[9] Moreover, in comprehensive treatments of Paul's theology, we are seeing union with Christ increasingly and rightly placed as the soteriological umbrella within which every facet of salvation is subsumed.[10] But have we sufficiently

---

8   E.g., Lewis B. Smedes, *Union with Christ: A Biblical View of the New Life in Jesus Christ*, 2nd ed. (Grand Rapids, MI: Eerdmans, 2009); J. Todd Billings, *Union with Christ: Reframing Theology and Ministry for the Church* (Grand Rapids, MI: Baker Academic, 2011); Robert Letham, *Union with Christ: In Scripture, History, and Theology* (Phillipsburg, NJ: P&R, 2011); Rankin Wilbourne, *Union with Christ: The Way to Know and Enjoy God* (Colorado Springs: Cook, 2018).

9   E.g., Constantine R. Campbell, *Paul and Union with Christ: An Exegetical and Theological Study* (Grand Rapids, MI: Zondervan Academic, 2012); Richard B. Gaffin Jr., *By Faith, Not by Sight: Paul and the Order of Salvation*, 2nd ed. (Phillipsburg, NJ: P&R, 2013), esp. 40–45; Grant Macaskill, *Living in Union with Christ: Paul's Gospel and Christian Moral Identity* (Grand Rapids, MI: Baker Academic, 2019).

10 E.g., Herman Ridderbos, *Paul: An Outline of His Theology*, trans. John Richard de Witt (Grand Rapids, MI: Eerdmans, 1975); James D. G. Dunn, *The Theology of Paul the Apostle* (Grand Rapids, MI: Eerdmans, 1998), esp. the comments on 399; G. K. Beale, *New Testament Biblical Theology: The Unfolding of the Old Testament in the New* (Grand Rapids, MI: Baker Academic, 2011); Moo, *Theology of Paul*.

emphasized the Spiritual union and solidarity that those who have been united to Christ vertically *now share with one another horizontally*?

As Paul puts it in 1 Corinthians 12:26, "If one member suffers, all suffer together; if one member is honored, all rejoice together." As he puts it in Romans 12:15, "Rejoice with those who rejoice, weep with those who weep." But in 2 Corinthians we see a more sustained emphasis on the union of believers with one another by virtue of their union with Christ. In some sense that we ought not press too far, believers are not only *in Christ* but also *in one another*. Because horizontal union is grounded in vertical union, horizontal union as believers is properly theological. At the very least, this means that self-concern and others-concern are far less distinguishable for Paul than for us and our natural, fallen ways of thinking.

One other way in 2 Corinthians 7 in which Paul expresses his interpersonal bond with the Corinthians with a self-conscious theological orientation is 7:12: "Although I wrote to you, it was not for the sake of the one who did the wrong, nor for the sake of the one who suffered the wrong, but in order that your earnestness for us might be revealed to you in the sight of God." Note once more the way Paul places the Paul/Corinthian mutual concern in the broader context of God himself ("in the sight of God"; cf. 4:2; 12:19). In every Christian fellowship, there are not merely two parties but three, God himself being the one *before whom* ("in the sight of") and, as we have been seeing above, *in whom*, the believers are relating.

Giving as a Reflection of Spiritual Solidarity with Other Believers (2 Corinthians 8–9)

We move now to 2 Corinthians 8–9. Space constraints prevent a full exegesis, but I will sketch out a few observations that further underscore what we have been seeing in the present chapter on Christian friendship and fellowship.

The overarching point of 2 Corinthians 8–9 is to garner financial aid from the Corinthian church for the Jerusalem Christians. Paul begins by using the Macedonian Christians' generosity (despite their own severe poverty) as an example. Throughout, Paul grounds Christian friendship theologically. His first words in this section refer to the Macedonians' generosity as "the grace of God that has been given among the churches of Macedonia" (8:1), grounding the horizontal reality of Christian care for other Christians in divine grace. Indeed, throughout this section of his epistle, Paul refers to financial generosity among believers as a matter of "grace" (8:4, 6, 7, 19) and bookends the whole discussion by closing his exhortation to generosity and speaking of it in terms of divine grace (9:14–15).

We note then the profound way in which Paul describes the friendship and concern flowing from the Macedonians to the Jerusalem Christians, despite the two parties almost certainly never having met. The Macedonians were "begging us earnestly for the favor [the word is, as in 8:1 and 8:6, 'grace,' *charis*] of taking part in the relief of the saints" (8:4). Paul continues by expressing his happy surprise at the Macedonian generosity and expresses theologically what they had done: "and this, not as we expected, but they gave themselves first to the Lord and then by the will of God to us" (8:5). This sounds quite similar to the Spiritual union and solidarity we observed in 2 Corinthians 7. The Corinthians were not simply handing over money; they had yielded themselves completely to the Lord (that is, to Jesus Christ) and then, as if by necessary implication, to Paul and company (this is why Paul tells the Corinthians toward the end of the letter that "I seek not what is yours but you," 12:14). *To give oneself to Christ is to give oneself to other believers, because our Spiritual union with Christ necessarily includes a derivative Spiritual union with other believers.* This union with other believers is, of course, non-salvific but no less vital.

Paul motivates the Corinthians to give generously by putting the gospel in financial terms (8:9), further grounding theologically the Corinthians' friendship with the Jerusalem believers (similarly 9:8). The second and final point I wish to make about 2 Corinthians 8–9 moves in a somewhat different direction, however. We have been noting the way Paul theologically connects the Corinthian believers to the Jerusalem believers. But we should also note simply the way in which Paul moves toward the Corinthians with this request—he does it *with friends*. Not only do we see Paul continue the first-person plural ("we"/"us") throughout, but we also see a recurring emphasis on team ministry as Paul collaborates with his friends and fellow leaders:

> We urged Titus that as he had started, so he should complete among you this act of grace. (8:6)

> Thanks be to God, who put into the heart of Titus the same earnest care I have for you. For he not only accepted our appeal, but being himself very earnest he is going to you of his own accord. With him we are sending the brother who is famous among all the churches for his preaching of the gospel. And not only that, but he has been appointed by the churches to travel with us as we carry out this act of grace that is being ministered by us, for the glory of the Lord himself and to show our good will. (8:16–19)

> And with them we are sending our brother whom we have often tested and found earnest in many matters, but who is now more earnest than ever because of his great confidence in you. (8:22)

> As for Titus, he is my partner and fellow worker for your benefit. And as for our brothers, they are messengers of the churches, the glory of Christ. So give proof before the churches of your love and of our boasting about you to these men. (8:23–24)

> I am sending the brothers so that our boasting about you may not prove empty in this matter, so that you may be ready, as I said you would be. Otherwise, if some Macedonians come with me and find that you are not ready, we would be humiliated—to say nothing of you—for being so confident. So I thought it necessary to urge the brothers to go on ahead to you and arrange in advance for the gift you have promised, so that it may be ready as a willing gift, not as an exaction. (9:3–5)

They [the Jerusalem church] will glorify God because of your sub-
mission that comes from your confession of the gospel of Christ,
and the generosity of your contribution for them and for all others,
while they long for you and pray for you. (9:13–14)

When we self-consciously wear a hermeneutical lens of friendship
or Christian camaraderie, we see this entire section of the letter replete
with this theme. This motif continues through the rest of the letter, such
as in 11:9, where Paul speaks of his intimate alliance with "the brothers
who came from Macedonia" who "supplied my need." But chapters 8
and 9 are conspicuous in how friendship shapes and informs the entire discussion of fundraising. Titus is Paul's key partner throughout,
though other ministry comrades are also being sent to Corinth on Paul's
behalf—the brother famed for his preaching (8:17) and the brother
tested and earnest (8:22). The presenting issue in 2 Corinthians 8–9 is
money, as important a matter for Christian reflection as any. But we
have focused on the underlying matters of deeper theological import
for Paul: (1) the way in which Paul theologically grounds financial
generosity among believers in divine grace and their joint solidarity in
Christ and (2) the way in which Paul's own ministry strategies involve
interpersonal cohesion rather than independence.

Conclusion

In this chapter we have considered the friendship motif in 2 Corinthians and have noted the way in which the glorious doctrine of union
with Christ has, as its necessary concomitant, Spiritual union and
solidarity with other believers. We close by noting that these explorations flow seamlessly with what we have been seeing in 2 Corinthians
more broadly.

For example, we considered in chapter 2 of the present study the
corporate solidarity that exists reciprocally between Christ and believers. We looked at 2 Corinthians 5:14: "One has died for all, therefore all
have died." We now see more deeply what this means, particularly with
regard to that final phrase that "all have died." Christ died the death

we all deserve to die, and in that death we are freed from the eternal penalty we otherwise deserve. That is the glorious vertical reality. But this vertical reality has as its corollary the joint horizontal reality that all believers have, together, died.

And we must note that this brief study of friendship in 2 Corinthians reflects the broader controlling reality of this letter and of the entire New Testament, the dawning of the new creational realm that Christ's past work launched and that the Spirit's present work proves. This is not to suggest that Old Testament saints did not enjoy friendship! But the theological grounding for interpersonal solidarity and union has been plunged down more deeply and wonderfully than ever before. For we believers are indwelt by the Spirit and united to Christ and thus enjoy a union with one another that transcends anything achievable by those out of Christ.

Christian togetherness, new realm friendship, is the freedom of sharing everything that we are and have with those to whom we are, in Christ, united. As Paul movingly puts it: "Our heart is wide open" (2 Cor. 6:11). Christian friendship is not utilitarian or pragmatic. It is the opening of one's heart in sincere service of the other. Following the example of Jesus Christ himself and empowered by his own dying friendship for us (John 15:12–15; 2 Cor. 5:21; 8:9; 13:4), this is the posture of Christian fellowship.

6

Heaven

The Hope of New Realm Ministry

WE TURN NOW TO THE AFTERLIFE. Logically it may make more
sense to save this for the last chapter. But I would like to close out the
book in chapter 7 with a reflection on the theme of strength in weakness, as that is the most pervasive, explicit theme of 2 Corinthians,
forming with inaugurated eschatology the twin hermeneutical keys
to understanding the letter.

The first point to make in moving to the theme of heaven and the
afterlife is that, in the broadest sense, this chapter is simply reflecting
on the "not yet" that complements the "already" that permeates the
entire letter of 2 Corinthians. We have been noting the way in which
inaugurated eschatology is the subterranean structure of 2 Corinthians,
and in coming to consider the afterlife we are moving to the consum-
mated eschatology that will bring final completion to that which was
inaugurated in Christ's first coming.

The second matter to take up is a clarification: I am using *heaven*
in the chapter title as shorthand for "the afterlife." As we will see, in
2 Corinthians and throughout the New Testament, heaven is where
believers spend a temporary period of time until Christ returns. Heaven
is not the believer's final destiny. But we also will see Paul describe an
experience of heaven in *this* life in 2 Corinthians, as well as discuss

the afterlife for *un*believers. So I am using the word *heaven* somewhat loosely in this chapter title.

Let's be more specific, given the broad lack of clarity among modern readers as to the way Paul and the New Testament writers understand our future. Taking the whole New Testament into view, we can think of a Christian's life in terms of four phases:

Phase 1: Out of Christ
Phase 2: In Christ but not with Christ
Phase 3: In Christ and with Christ, but disembodied
Phase 4: In Christ and with Christ, and embodied

Let's make this concrete for clarity. For the sake of argument, let's say a man is converted to Christ at age thirty, dies at age eighty, and Christ returns in judgment one hundred years after that. In this case, this man spends thirty years in phase 1, fifty years in phase 2, one hundred years in phase 3, and an eternity in phase 4. We could further nuance this in a number of ways. For example, Paul is clear that our election takes place in Christ (Eph. 1:4; 2 Tim. 1:9). So from one vantage point, we saints are actually "in Christ" far earlier than our conversion to Christ in this life. But the basic structure remains, whatever cosmetic tweaks we may wish to add to this schema.

The point here is twofold. One, we are noting the escalating way in which believers are brought to restored humanity, phase by phase, as those united to Christ. Two, we see that our final future is not disembodied but embodied. In phases 2 and 3, believers are raised spiritually but not yet physically. We could put it this way: phase 1 is bad; phase 2 is good; phase 3 is better; and phase 4 is best. I have taken the word "better" as a useful starting point due to Philippians 1, where Paul is torn between staying and working here on earth or departing to be with Christ, and Paul calls going immediately to be with Christ "far better." It is reasonable to understand Paul as referring to the intermediate state, in which believers are with Christ as living souls but still awaiting the final bodily resurrection when Christ returns to earth. The intermediate state is the period of time from a believer's death to the return of Christ and the attendant bodily resurrection of both believers and unbelievers.[1] The current recovery in evangelical scholarship of believers' final future as this-worldly and embodied ought not to obfuscate the reality of an intermediate state nor to dilute the spiritual and soulish side of human sinfulness and divine redemption.[2]

The Afterlife in 2 Corinthians: Three Brief Texts

These brief introductory remarks are meant simply as an entryway into 2 Corinthians and its contribution to how we think about the afterlife, clearing up some common ambiguities about the Bible's teaching on our future.

Paul mentions the afterlife in at least six passages in 2 Corinthians.[3] Three of these are passing mentions (1:14; 4:14; 11:15) and three of them are more sustained reflections (4:16–18; 5:1–10; 12:1–4). We'll take the briefer texts first.

In 1:14 Paul is drawing out the Corinthians' otherwise tepid love for him, bringing them into deeper relational solidarity with him. His concluding remark expresses his hope and longing "that on the day of our Lord Jesus you will boast of us as we will boast of you." The reference to "the day of our Lord Jesus" is a typically Pauline transmutation of an Old Testament theme that refers to the day of the Lord or Yahweh into a new phrase that makes Christ the referent. The "day of the Lord" anticipated in the Old Testament was the anticipated coming of God to restore and vindicate his people. While

---

1 I am seeking here and throughout this chapter to be as inclusive as possible with regard to different millennial schemes.

2 Richard Middleton makes both mistakes in *A New Heaven and a New Earth: Reclaiming Biblical Eschatology* (Grand Rapids, MI: Baker Academic, 2014). A better guide for these matters would be Herman Bavinck, *Holy Spirit, Church, and New Creation*, vol. 4 of *Reformed Dogmatics*, ed. J. Bolt, trans. J. Vriend (Grand Rapids, MI: Baker Academic, 2008), esp. 589–643.

3 It is possible that Paul has the afterlife in mind in two further texts (1:10; 2:16), but I will pass on looking at these given how difficult it is to know if Paul has the future life in mind.

the decisive inauguration of this day has occurred in the first coming of Christ, Paul tends to retain the language of "the day" to refer to the future consummation, at Christ's second coming, of what began at Christ's first coming. The particular phrase "the day of our Lord Jesus" is a variation on a common way in which Paul refers to the future return of Jesus to earth.[4]

What interests us specifically is how Paul describes what will happen on that day. Among other things, when Jesus returns, the Corinthians will apparently boast of Paul, and Paul will boast of the Corinthians. The double expression is intriguing and suggestive but perhaps a bit elusive, especially as it is referring to a future event for which none of us currently have a category. The language of "boasting" is pervasive in 2 Corinthians, more so by far than in any other Pauline letter. The motif is especially thick on the ground in chapters 10–13, as Paul upends our natural fallen impulse to boast in worldly ways and instead commends a way of life in which believers boast in their weaknesses, thereby displaying Christ's strength. But the theme begins even here toward the beginning of the letter. And the point in 1:14 seems to be that on the day when Jesus returns, there will be a beautiful mutual rejoicing over one another—the Corinthians celebrating Paul's spiritual fathering that has fostered their life in Christ (1 Cor. 4:15) and Paul celebrating the progress, maturing, and fruitfulness of his beloved spiritual children. Authentic Christianity, contrary to the spirit at Corinth,[5] does not boast in oneself but in one another—that is, in those believers whom we have discipled and who have discipled us. That, for healthy Christians, is the great heart thrill when Jesus returns. Whatever Christ's parousia means for the saints individually—and it means a lot, as we are cleansed from sin, given a resurrection body, judged according to our works, see Christ, leave all pain behind, and more—it also includes a wonderful rejoicing

---

4   See the listing of ten different variations on this phrase in Paul, and the attendant discussion, in Douglas J. Moo, *A Theology of Paul and His Letters: The Gift of the New Realm in Christ*, BTNT (Grand Rapids, MI: Zondervan Academic, 2021), 534–36.

5   On which see chapter 7 below.

over our fellow Christians and a particular exulting in those with whom we have stumbled forward in this brief life, arms around one another, pursuing Christ.[6]

In 4:13–15 Paul is expressing the way faith affects how we "speak," and in 4:16–18 he will reflect on how faith affects our "heart." Paul grounds our confidence with regard to the former in what we know— namely, "that he who raised the Lord Jesus will raise us also with Jesus and bring us with you into his presence" (4:14). The reference is clearly to the future return of Christ. Whereas Paul mentions in 1:14 the mutual horizontal boasting that will take place on that day, at 4:14 he speaks of the bodily resurrecting that we will enjoy on that day. It is worth observing the phrase "with Jesus," without which the sentence would still have made sense. But Paul includes the phrase to underscore the solidarity between believers and Jesus in the na-ture of the resurrection body we will experience. The kind of body Christ received upon resurrection is the kind of body his people will receive. Just because he is also divine does not mean his physical body is different than ours in the resurrected state. We might also note in passing the way in which Paul is not content merely to mention the bodily resurrection of him and the Corinthians but also the attendant ushering of all of them into the very presence of Christ, once more driving home the solidarity and union believers enjoy (as explored in chapter 5 above).

The third text is 11:15. We saw earlier in chapter 4 that according to 11:14 "Satan disguises himself as an angel of light." Paul then makes the application to the super-apostles: "So it is no surprise if his servants, also, disguise themselves as servants of righteousness" (11:15). What concerns us at the moment is the following description of their fate: "Their end will correspond to their deeds" (a new sentence in the ESV

---

6 This is the text (2 Cor. 1:14) on which Jonathan Edwards preached his famous farewell sermon in 1750, bracingly telling the church that had just fired him that they would meet once more at the judgment seat of Christ when he returns. Jonathan Edwards, "A Farewell Sermon," in *The Sermons of Jonathan Edwards: A Reader*, ed. D. A. Sweeney, K. P. Minkema, and W. H. Kimnach (New Haven: Yale University Press, 2008), 212–40.

but a seamless continuation of the sentence in the Greek: "whose end will be according to their deeds"). Paul does not explicitly speak of the afterlife here; he does not mention *geenna* (Gehenna, hell), but simply unbelievers' "end" (*telos*). It is possible that Paul has in mind some sort of judicial or retributive end in this life, but more likely he is referring to the next life and the accordant judgment that their evil deeds deserve. Below we will need to wrestle with how this is different from the fate of believers, who are saved by grace and yet are also judged according to their deeds (2 Cor. 5:10).

The Afterlife in 2 Corinthians: Three Longer Passages

Having looked briefly at three passing references to the afterlife, we turn to three more sustained texts. Beginning with 4:16–18, we find ourselves in one of the most beautiful and consoling texts of Scripture.[7] Paul continues his theme of the life of the new realm that even now has broken in on the death characterizing the old realm, but now he turns from looking in at his own experience (4:7–12) and from looking out to others (4:13–15) to looking ahead to believers' inevitable and incomparable future (4:16–18).

2 Corinthians 4:16–18

Paul repeats a phrase from 4:1, bringing the argument within these two bookends full circle: "We do not lose heart" (4:16). This has been Paul's driving point—to encourage his readers. Yet it is an encouragement that does not shy away from the manifest reasons we find all around us to lose heart. Rather, Paul weds utter realism with soaring hope, resulting in a stability and calm as we weather the billows of life. We see this realism when he acknowledges, "Our outer self is wasting away" (4:16). To waste away means to decay, to erode bit by bit—it's the same verb (*diaphtheirō*) used in Luke 12:33 to speak of what moths do to treasure over time, eating away at it bit by bit. But what is "the outer

---

7   Portions of what follows for these final three passages have been adapted from Dane Ortlund, *2 Corinthians*, in *Romans–Galatians*, vol. 10 of *ESV Expository Commentary* (Wheaton, IL: Crossway, 2020), 461–70, 545–50. Used by permission.

self"? It is critical to note here that the Greek text is "outer *man*" (*ho exō hēmōn anthrōpos*). It is the entire human being according to the old age. It is the remnant of us that remains but is decaying, belonging to the old order. Picture a healthy cicada (a large flying insect native to the United States) struggling to break out of its decaying outer shell. The outer shell is still there, part of the insect; but it does not define it. It is falling away. Soon it will be no part of the new life the cicada has already begun to experience.

Accordingly, the "inner self" (i.e., "inner man," *ho esō*; Paul drops *anthrōpos*, but it is clearly implied, parallel to "the outer man") is the "you" that belongs to the new age—the real you, the eternal you, the you in Christ. And the real you, by the Spirit, in union with the resurrected Christ, is taking one step closer to the consummation of your destiny day by day. The shell is crumbling away, doomed to perish. But the new you is waking up, fresh and strong and beginning to stretch its limbs, preparing—not yet physically, but spiritually—for the life of the new earth.[8]

Having spoken of the outer man (belonging to the old age) decaying and the inner man (belonging to the new age) striding forward, Paul pauses to return momentarily to the outer (old age) man. What is this "wasting away" actually accomplishing? His answer is "an eternal weight of glory beyond all comparison" (4:17), and here we arrive at the explicit reference to the afterlife in this passage. And what is added here is the incomparable resplendence with which all those in Christ will be clothed.[9] Elsewhere in his letters Paul speaks of the glory in which believers themselves will be draped as an implication of their union with the glorious Christ (1 Thess. 2:12; 2 Thess. 1:12). The glory that begins now as we are glorified in an inaugurated way in this life (i.e., the image is decisively reinstated as we are united to *the* image of

8   For more on understanding "the outer man" and "the inner man" in 2 Cor. 4:16, see the incisive analysis of Richard B. Gaffin Jr., *By Faith, Not by Sight: Paul and the Order of Salvation*, 2nd ed. (Phillipsburg, NJ: P&R, 2013), 61–66.

9   C. S. Lewis reflects speculatively but gloriously on "the weight of glory" in the essay of that name: "The Weight of Glory," in *The Weight of Glory and Other Addresses* (New York: Touchstone, 1975), 25–40.

God, Jesus Christ; see Rom. 8:29–30) is brought to radiant consummation in the next life.[10]

A further underscoring of the eschatological undercurrents at play in 2 Corinthians 4:16–18 may not be immediately apparent in English translation. "Beyond all comparison" is literally "a surpassing unto surpassing eternality"—that is, a new age eternality (*aiōnios*, related to *aiōn*, "age") that is characterized by a quality of glory that cannot be compared to even the best glories of this present evil age. We note how "heavenly minded" Paul is here—he can call the sufferings of this life "slight" (or "light"; the only other New Testament occurrence of the word, *elaphros*, is Jesus's comment that his burden is "light" in Matt. 11:30). This is the same Paul who catalogued his profound and unique anguishes at length multiple times in this very letter (2 Cor. 6:3–10; 11:23–29). How can he call these sufferings light? Not because he was a masochist or even a stoic. But in comparison to the coming glory, they are light as a feather. For they are "momentary." The coming heavy weight of glory is "eternal." See then the two pairs of opposites Paul employs in contrasting the pains of this world with the glory of the next: light versus heavy, temporary versus eternal. In weight the two can't be compared because in length of time the two can't be compared.

Paul continues one of these pairs into 4:18: the temporary/eternal contrast. The first half of the verse explains how we apprehend what he has just described, the simultaneous powering down of the old man and the renewing of the new man. Paul uses the metaphor of sight, already present in the context through the pervasive use of the veil imagery. But among the several sight-related verbs Paul could have chosen, he uses one (*skopeō*) that includes a connotation of to "look out" or "watch out" or, as we might say today, "keep your eyes peeled" (cf. the other four Pauline uses: Rom. 16:17; Gal. 6:1; Phil. 2:4; 3:17). Paul is saying that our present afflictions are nurturing future glory (2 Cor. 4:17) and that we become attuned to that and heartened by it as

---

10   See Dane C. Ortlund, "Inaugurated Glorification: Revisiting Romans 8:30," *JETS* 57, no. 1 (2014): 111–33.

we pay close attention to the invisible rather than the visible world. The paradox is plain: we are to look at what can't be looked at. That is, we are to fix our heart's eyes (cf. Eph. 1:18) on the next world, the coming glory—invisible to physical eyes, apprehended only by the eyes of faith.

The second half of 2 Corinthians 4:18 picks up this "things seen" / "things not seen" contrast and connects it to the temporary/eternal contrast of 4:17: "For the things that are seen are transient." "Transient" echoes "momentary" from 4:17. It's the only time Paul uses the word; this is the word used in the parable of the sower to describe the seed that had no root and fell away when adversity came (Matt. 13:21; Mark 4:17). He continues, "But the things that are unseen are eternal." Using the word *aiōnios* again ("eternal"; also 2 Cor. 4:17), Paul says that we fix our eyes on the invisible world because this is the one that lasts. And it is here now. Nowhere in this passage does Paul say the things seen are present and the things unseen are future, as if our final state is an ethereal, disembodied one. To be sure, one day the invisible will explode visibly onto world history, far more solid and concrete than the most visible realities today (Rev. 21:1–5). But we are fixing our minds on the coming embodiment of the new age that has already quietly erupted onto world history in Christ's resurrection and our co-resurrection through union with him (cf. Col. 3:1–4).

2 Corinthians 5:1–10

This is perhaps Scripture's clearest teaching on the intermediate state— that is, the period of time between a Christian's death and the return of Christ. This is the time when a Christian is in the awkward position of not having a body, and this awkwardness is what Paul is exploring in this passage for the Corinthians' encouragement. And yet even this interme- diate state is not Paul's main point but a reality he raises in the course of talking about something much better: our final resurrection body.

Throughout the passage, Paul uses two images: houses and cloth- ing. We see here as clearly as anywhere in Scripture the way in which a Christian's life has progressively successive stages: an earthly life out of Christ, an earthly life in Christ, the intermediate state, and then final resurrection.[11] Because of the interpretive challenges of this text, the unique teaching it gives on the afterlife, and the central role it plays in 2 Corinthians, I will give it more sustained consideration than other texts.

Paul has recounted numerous flirtations with death thus far in the epistle, but every time he has escaped (1:9–10; 4:9–12). Now he explores, for the Corinthians' comfort, what would happen if he did not. He is continuing his reasoning from 4:16–18 for why we do not lose heart despite the powering down of the frail body that belongs fundamentally to the old age. Paul introduces in 5:1 the imagery of a "tent" and a "house" in reassuring his readers of the final resurrection body that is to come when Christ returns and establishes the new heavens and the new earth, a promise so sure that Paul can say "we have" it, using the present tense. As a tentmaker himself (Acts 18:3), Paul was well familiar with tents. The Corinthians would understand what Paul meant when he spoke of this earthly body, this "jar of clay" (2 Cor. 4:7), as a tent. What awaits us instead is something far more substantial, a "house" defined by three characteristics: "from God," "not made with hands," and "eternal in the heavens" (probably referring not to a location in heaven but its heavenly nature). All three marks speak to the divine source of the future resurrection body as sheer grace and something only God himself can create.

But Paul is saying something deeper for those who have ears to hear. The three key word roots in 2 Corinthians 5:1 appear in one other New Testament text: Mark 14:58. There Jesus is accused before the Jewish council of claiming, "I will destroy this temple that is made with hands, and in three days *I will build* another, not made with hands." The three Greek words underlying "I will destroy," "I will build," and "not made with human hands" are the same ones found in 2 Corinthians 5:1. And

---

11 This is a notoriously tricky passage to unfold in terms of the sequence of events in the future. For a thorough discussion of the options, see Murray J. Harris, *The Second Epistle to the Corinthians*, NIGTC (Grand Rapids, MI: Eerdmans, 2005), 369–84. The view taken in the present discussion can be found further explained in G. K. Beale, *New Testament Biblical Theology: The Unfolding of the Old Testament in the New* (Grand Rapids, MI: Baker Academic, 2011), 270–74.

as we know from the parallel to Mark 14:58 in John 2:19–22, Jesus is speaking in temple terms. Paul's use of these three terms can hardly be coincidental, and it seems likely that he is drawing on temple categories to speak of believers' final future. This is all the more likely in light of Paul's use of "tent" language (*skēnos*)—the same Greek word used throughout the Septuagint to speak of the tabernacle.

The point of 5:1, then, is that even as this earthly body wears out and dies, we know that we are only moved more invincibly into the spiritual eschatological temple of which Jesus is the cornerstone (Eph. 2:19–22), a point we have already explored above in chapter 1 in reflecting on 2 Corinthians 6:16. We enjoy more deeply the fellowship with God himself that the temple was meant to facilitate all along.

In 2 Corinthians 5:2 Paul acknowledges the painful, grinding existence as "jars of clay" (4:7). This is more than back pain, erosion of cartilage in our knees, gradual hearing loss, and decreasing energy levels. Though not less than such things, these are symptoms of a deeper groaning: the groaning from within fueled by the acute knowledge that we are made for immortality. That our bodies would begin to power down from about age thirty feels bizarre, foreign, out of place. Death comes to all, but despite its universality we know deep within that it is unnatural.[12] Paul's only other use of the word "groan" outside of 2 Corinthians 5:2 and 5:4 is Romans 8:23, speaking of our groaning and longing for our resurrection bodies in the new earth. "Our heavenly dwelling," we remember, is not a reference to the intermediate state in heaven but the final "heavenly" body we will receive in the new earth (cf. Paul's use of "heavenly" in speaking of this body in 1 Cor. 15:40–41, 44, 46).

Paul is not raising a question with the "if indeed" in 2 Corinthians 5:3 but driving assurance even deeper ("since it is true that"). Paul had raised the language of clothing in 5:2 for the first time with "to put on" (*ependyomai*), and he continues that metaphor here, using a synonymous verb (*endyō*). As those in Christ, we long to be dressed in

---

12 Cf. Bavinck: "All peoples take for granted that humans are by nature immortal and that it is death, not immortality, that requires explanation. It is death that seems an unnatural thing." Bavinck, *Holy Spirit, Church, and New Creation*, 590.

the same immortal resurrection body that Christ himself now wears. The use of clothing imagery should not be pushed too far; Paul is not saying that the new body is only an external affair, as if it merely covers a present mortality underneath. The change is far more drastic, and 2 Corinthians 5:1–10 should be interpreted in conjunction with 1 Corinthians 15:12–49 in order to maintain the right balance between continuity and discontinuity from this earthly body to the resurrection body. To be clothed with a resurrection body is for the mortal to put on immortality—a comprehensive, total transformation (1 Cor. 15:54), while still identifiable with the body and identity of one's mortal existence.[13] Paul's point in 2 Corinthians 5:3 is that there will be no awkwardness or embarrassment when we put on our future resurrection body. The reference to nakedness in 5:3 may be speaking of the intermediate state, but in light of the way Paul uses this word (*gymnos*) in a strongly parallel passage (1 Cor. 15:37), it more likely refers to this mortal existence. We are *now* "naked," compared to the glorious risen body awaiting us. This naked body is a mere seed that will be sown upon death, only to be raised immortal (1 Cor. 15:35–37, 42–44).

In 2 Corinthians 5:4 Paul picks up the train of thought from 5:2, speaking again of this earthly "tent" in which "we groan." Here he probes further the cause of our groaning. The word he uses is *bareō* (as a present participle): "being burdened." It's the same word Paul used in 1:8 to speak of being utterly overwhelmed at the near-death experience in Asia; it's also used in the Gospels to speak of the disciples' eyes being heavy with sleep (Matt. 26:43). The meaning in 2 Corinthians 5:4 is that existence in this mortal frame is cumbersome, weighed down, laborious. As those who remain existing in the old realm, we find ourselves dragged downward; the body to come in the new realm will know no such burden.

But Paul feels he must immediately qualify what he is saying, perhaps due to a Corinthian gnostic proclivity to privilege the immaterial over

---

13 N. T. Wright suggests the term "transphysical" to describe the risen state in *The Resurrection of the Son of God*, vol. 3 of Christian Origins and the Question of God (Minneapolis: Fortress, 2003), 477.

the material. "Not that we would be unclothed" (5:4)—that is, it isn't as if we want a final state that is disembodied. Just because we groan now as we lug around this bag of flesh doesn't mean that our desire is to be free of a body altogether. That may have been a Greek ideal but was not a Hebrew one. God created the body. It is good (Gen. 1:26–31). Good but fallen. Paul's longing is not for a bodiless existence but a sinless existence. Our longing is therefore to "be further clothed"—to trade in the bodily "clothing" of this present age for that of the age to come. In this way "what is mortal may be swallowed up by life," the life of the age to come, eschatological life, the deepest longing of a believer's heart. This life will be so comprehensive, so utterly complete, that all our present weaknesses and mortality will be "swallowed up" (used also in 2 Cor. 2:7 of the sinner whom Paul wishes not to be "swallowed up" or "overwhelmed" by sorrow).

We have already expounded the significance of 2 Corinthians 5:5, where Paul assures believers that they have already received the down payment of the Spirit. So we will not linger over this text except to note once more the way the life of the new realm that Paul is exploring in 5:1–10 has now taken root in believers.

Ever the pastor, Paul makes the connection between his teaching on the afterlife with the "courage" it naturally fosters (5:6; cf. 4:1, 16). He then grounds this courage by introducing the language of being "at home" or "away" either "in the body" or "from/with the Lord." The meaning of "at home" is to dwell contently in one's native homeland, and to "be away" is accordingly to be living abroad as an exile.[14] The apostle's point is that because Christ in his spiritual resurrection body has gone ahead of us to heaven, we his people are not in his immediate presence. We are *in* him; but we are not *with* him, at least in the fullest sense (we do have his Spirit within us, which renders certain that we will finally be with him).

Second Corinthians 5:7 continues the thought: "For we walk by faith, not by sight." This is a classic Pauline statement of what it means

14 See "ἐκδημέω," BDAG 300.

to be drawn into the new realm. Paul's next words explain what it looks like for us here and now to live as those united to Christ, indwelt by his Spirit, but not yet with Christ our beloved Lord. These words have rightly been held dear by generations of Christians. But we must understand what Paul is saying in the flow of his argument. He is not offering a bare truism to be remembered anytime something confusing unfolds in our lives. Rather, Paul is describing the mental "neutral" of ordinary, daily existence as those united to Christ to be *eschatologically informed*. When did Paul last speak of "faith"? Back in 4:13, where the "spirit of faith" leads one to "believe" that the same God who raised Jesus will also raise those in him. But this is not a "faith" opposed to "knowledge." Both in 4:13–14 and 5:6–7, it is a faith grounded in knowledge (note "knowing" in 4:14 and "we know" in 5:6). To "walk by faith," then, is to proceed through life keenly mindful that one day soon we will join Christ in enjoying the resurrection body of which the Spirit is the first installment.

In 5:6 Paul reiterates the "good courage" we know here and now as we walk by faith, assured of the resurrection body to come in light of the inbreaking of the eschaton decisively now as proven in the presence of the Spirit. Then he says something that is easily misunderstood. When he asserts that "we would rather be away from the body and at home with the Lord" (5:8), he is making a statement *not about the inferiority of bodily existence but of the superior value of Christ and being with him.* If Paul has to choose between being in this mortal body or with the resurrected Lord, the choice is clear (cf. Phil. 1:23). But, happily, the broader contours of this passage teach that ultimately a believer need not make this choice. We will, finally, have both: a glorious resurrected body with the Lord.

We know that we will one day be with him, "at home" (5:9). But even here, walking by faith, we "make it our aim" to please Christ. The verb used here (*philotimeomai*; also in Rom. 15:20; 1 Thess. 4:11) means to place as one's all-trumping concern, into which all other competing concerns of life funnel. Paul is saying that in light of the divinely initiated guarantee of resurrection life in the presence of the one who died for us and has been raised into the kind of immortal existence that is our own certain future, what else would we do but long to please him? But there is also a more sobering reason we aim to please Christ. We will one day stand before him as he renders judgment over our lives—"all" of us (5:10). Does a statement such as this (of which there are several; the closest to 2 Cor. 5:10 is Rom. 14:10) contradict Paul's teaching on justification by faith? By no means. Here we can only sketch a few lines of thought.[15]

First, the verb Paul uses, translated as "he has done," is not the more common word for "do" (*poieō*) but the rarer *prassō*, which means to practice or make a habit of doing (cf. the other use at 2 Cor. 12:21). While our lives will be judged comprehensively, this is not a nitpicky judgment. God knows we are weak and prone to err. It is a judgment of the whole of our life, the trajectories we set, the patterns, the habits. This is reinforced by the final phrase of the verse: "whether good or evil." Paul's use of the singular for "good" and "evil" likewise signals general trajectories of life.

Second, that this judgment is not only for "evil" but also for "good" suggests that Paul is speaking of *rewards* that follow and do not threaten the decisive justifying verdict over our lives. Even these rewards, we remember from Augustine, are gifts of God's own grace and not our own self-generated virtue.[16] But God in his great kindness deigns to dignify us for our good works even though he is ultimately responsible for them (cf. 9:8).

Third, we bear in mind the context. Paul has been instilling in his readers a deep awareness of the resurrection they have already begun to experience through the presence of the Spirit (5:5) as we carry around the resurrection life of Jesus (4:10–11). The deeds for which we are judged, we are heartened to know, are deeds not wrought out

---

15 More fully, see Dane C. Ortlund, "Justified by Faith, Judged according to Works: Another Look at a Pauline Paradox," *JETS* 52, no. 2 (2009): 323–39.

16 See Augustine, *On Grace and Free Will*, in vol. 5 of *Nicene and Post-Nicene Fathers*, Series 1, ed. Philip Schaff, trans. Peter Holmes and Robert Ernest Wallis (Grand Rapids, MI: Christian Classics Ethereal Library, n.d.), www.ccel.org.

of self-manufactured energies but out of the new life into which we have been irreversibly swept up. A life of good deeds is simply *living in accord with who we now are* as eschatological creatures.

Fourth, it is profoundly reassuring to know that the universe in which we find ourselves, despite appearances at times to the contrary, is a place of utter and final moral seriousness. As Paul teaches in Galatians 6:7–10, everyone reaps what he or she sows. God is not mocked (Gal. 6:7). Devious motives will be exposed (1 Cor. 4:5). Justice will be served. We can live at peace now, knowing that God will right all wrongs.

We move on to consider one more passage in 2 Corinthians that touches on the afterlife before synthesizing our findings.

2 Corinthians 12:1–4

This text, unique in the New Testament corpus, speaks of Paul being caught up to the third heaven. It fits with Paul's continued "boasting" as he demonstrates to the Corinthians that if he wanted, he could beat the super-apostles at their own game—but Paul's preferred method is to upend Corinthian sensibilities by boasting in his weaknesses.

This passage is a little mystifying, and we should proceed with caution as to whether, and how much, it builds on our understanding of the afterlife. Paul's experience is clearly a distinctive and unique one, which probably goes some way toward explaining his unique apostolic insights and understanding of God's ways through redemptive history (cf. Gal. 2:1–2). Nevertheless, a few comments are in order. This is, after all, the only place in 2 Corinthians other than 5:1–2 where Paul refers to "heaven" (*ouranos*).

As 2 Corinthians 12 opens, we hear Paul reaching back to an experience fourteen years prior. It is a moment so sacred that Paul hardly knows how to describe it. One senses his sheepishness as he holds himself at a distance from the episode, speaking of himself in the third person ("I know a man," 12:2; "this man," 12:3, 5). (That it is Paul in view becomes clear in 12:5–7.) While God knows the exact nature of the experience, Paul expresses ignorance as to whether his experience was "in the body or out of the body." He repeats this in 12:3, presumably to drive the point home to the Corinthians that what precisely happened physiologically to him was irrelevant. It is salutary to remember that the church in Corinth was particularly prone to misunderstanding human anthropology and the relationship between the spirit and the body (e.g., 1 Cor. 2:11–16; 3:16–17; 6:12–19; 7:2–5; 8:8–9; 9:4–5; 11:21–22; 12:1; 15:35–49; 2 Cor. 4:16–18; 5:1–5; 6:14–7:1). Paul wants to prevent any distraction. He is telling them, and us today, not to worry about the specific psychosomatic nature of this experience. That would be to miss the more basic point he is after.

Paul says he was "caught up to the third heaven." What is he referring to? The number three is a number of wholeness or completion. Perhaps beyond this, Paul considered heaven to have three "levels" according to a cosmology inspired by Old Testament texts that speak of "heaven, even the highest heaven," which is literally "heaven and the heaven of heaven" (Deut. 10:14; 1 Kings 8:27; 2 Chron. 2:6; 6:18; Neh. 9:6). The point is that the apostle entered the very heart of heaven and, thus, the sublime presence of God himself. Paul gives one other descriptor of heaven: "paradise" (2 Cor. 12:3). This word (*paradeisos*) is used just two other times in the New Testament: Jesus telling the thief he would be with him that day "in paradise" (Luke 23:43) and a reference to "the paradise of God" in the next life in the letter to the church at Ephesus (Rev. 2:7).

The word "caught up" (*harpazō*) is a strong one, occurring fourteen times in the New Testament and often denoting being "snatched up" (e.g., John 10:28), even forcefully (e.g., Matt. 11:12). Paul did not climb a spiritual ladder to get there. He was divinely transported. This was a non-manipulatable—and, thus, presumably non-repeatable—experience.

We learn in 2 Corinthians 12:4 that, strikingly, it was not what Paul saw but what he heard that he focuses on as unrepeatable. He heard *arrēta rhēmata*, "un-word-able words." What he heard could not be replicated by mortal mouths. Not only this, but also what he heard should not be repeated: "which man may not utter."

When it comes to the afterlife, we learn from this passage that sometimes God may deign to give carefully restrained and appropriately selective excursions to heaven for the sake of the ongoing mission of the church and, at least in Paul's case, the accordant warding off of pride (12:7).

Synthesis

Let us put together what we have seen. Heaven is the place in which God resides, the "paradise" we all long for, and God at his choosing may even allow saints in this life to glimpse the glories of heaven (2 Cor. 12:1–4). But whether one sees heaven in this life or not, one day the Lord Jesus will return, and God's leaders will rejoice over those they have led while those they have led will rejoice over their leaders (1:14). Saints who die before Jesus returns will experience a disembodied intermediate state. This phase is better than our earthly existence, not because we lose our body but because we lose our sin. The best state of all is when we are "home," "further clothed" with a new body in the new earth (5:1–10). In that final state, we will be free of sin but also receive the resurrection body, the very resurrection of Jesus himself, and will be brought with our fellow Christians into the very presence of Jesus (4:14). The alternative to believers' future is unbelievers' future, in which the end will be according to one's deeds (11:15).

In the middle of the longest passage on the afterlife in 2 Corinthians (5:1–10), we have seen Paul speak of the Spirit as believers' "down payment" (5:5). The broadest reality under which we must understand the afterlife in 2 Corinthians is that—I state the point cautiously—*what we long for in the afterlife has already, in this life, begun.* The broadest rubric within which to read 2 Corinthians is inaugurated eschatology, and we must recognize that the message of 2 Corinthians and the New Testament is that heaven itself has taken root in the believer, though we still await the final completion of what has begun.

7

Strength through Weakness

The Secret to New Realm Ministry

LOGICALLY THE CASE COULD BE MADE to conclude this book with the chapter on heaven. But I have wanted to leave this theme of strength through weakness for the final chapter, as a bookend functioning in tandem with the opening chapter on inaugurated eschatology. This is because the theme of strength in weakness pervasively, conspicuously, and (relative to the rest of the New Testament) uniquely controls the letter of 2 Corinthians. It is also perhaps the most pastorally consoling of all the themes explored in the present volume, so it is fitting to close the book with this theme.

The Excesses of First-Century Corinth

This is a study of the theology of 2 Corinthians, but in this chapter that theology will be most usefully illuminated against the historical and cultural backdrop of first-century Corinth. So I begin by sketching out a few contours of the city of Corinth in Paul's day. One way to understand 2 Corinthians is that the city of Corinth is influencing the church at Corinth instead of the church at Corinth influencing the city of Corinth.

Combing ancient sources reveals at least five ways in which Corinth pursued what we might call *excess*, that fleshly indulgence that Paul inverts throughout 2 Corinthians. These ways are money, power, athleticism, speech, and sensuality. I gratefully acknowledge my debt here to Timothy Savage who, while focusing on 2 Corinthians 3–4, has brought out the cultural ethos of first-century Corinth in illuminating juxtaposition with Paul's letters to the Corinthian church.[1]

The first arena of excess was money. Corinth was destroyed in 146 BC, but Julius Caesar founded the city again as a Roman colony in 44 BC.[2] The strategically placed port city rapidly acquired what would become its lasting reputation, one element of which was its great wealth. Because merchants passing through were taxed on their goods, whether traveling by land or sea, Corinth grew economically quite quickly in the second half of the first century BC as the new Corinth regained and then outdistanced the economic status of the old.[3] This was fueled not only by location and taxing but also by the makeup of the citizens of the new Corinth. The city was largely settled by freedmen. In a free market in which upward mobility was the word of the day, this meant a highly competitive social drive fueled the activities of daily life in an unusually strong way when compared with other, older cities in which the social strata were more rigidly fixed.

Strabo passed through Corinth during the period in which it was being resettled (44 BC and on), and he tells us that Corinth "was always great and wealthy," elsewhere referring to the city simply as "wealthy Corinth."[4] This was evidently true not only of pre-destruction Corinth but supremely of the new city founded by Julius Caesar. For example,

1   Timothy B. Savage, *Power through Weakness: Paul's Understanding of the Christian Ministry in 2 Corinthians*, SNTSMS 86 (Cambridge: Cambridge University Press, 1996), 19–102.

2   *The Geography of Strabo*, vol. 4, *Books 8–9*, trans. Horace Leonard Jones, LCL (Cambridge, MA: Harvard University Press, 1927), 121, 203–5; F. F. Bruce, *New Testament History* (New York: Doubleday, 1969), 18.

3   Jerome Murphy-O'Connor, *St. Paul's Corinth: Texts and Archaeology* (Collegeville, MN: Liturgical, 2002), 86.

4   *The Geography of Strabo*, 185, 203.

Pliny the Elder (AD 23–79) lauded the distinctive worth of Corinthian bronze,[5] as did Josephus[6] and Livy.[7]

Second, the Corinthians prized power. What status was to secular Corinth, power was to religious Corinth. At the heart of Greco-Roman religion was the desire for a deity to show itself strong on behalf of its followers, thereby showing its adherents to be strong (cf. Acts 8:10).[8] Poseidon, god of the sea, was held in grave respect not because of his benevolence or generosity but his power.[9] Thus Cicero, after reflecting on the way in which some persons have been "deified" after they have "made some discovery of special utility for civilization," asks, "But what could be more ridiculous than to award divine honors to things mean and ugly, or to give the rank of gods to men now dead and gone?"[10] Similarly, Diogenes, according to Dio Chrysostom, "moved to Corinth, since he considered none of the others worth associating with," and noted the extreme gullibility of the Corinthians to any promise for physical healing and increased bodily strength.[11]

Third, the competitive status seeking that drove Corinth socially carried over into the athletic world. Corinth was especially influenced on this account by the Isthmian Games, held every other year beginning around 40 BC.[12] The economic strengthening brought in by the Isthmian Games meant that money and the athletic arena were mutually

5   *Pliny the Elder's Natural History*, vol. 9, *Books 33–35*, trans. H. Rackham, LCL (Cambridge, MA: Harvard University Press, 1913), 127, 131.

6   Josephus, *The Jewish War*, vol. 3, *Books 4–7*, trans. H. St. J. Thackeray, LCL (Cambridge, MA: Harvard University Press, 1928), 261. See also Josephus, *The Life*, trans. H. St. J. Thackeray, LCL (Cambridge, MA: Harvard University Press, 1926), 29.

7   *Livy, History of Rome*, vol. 9, *Books 31–34*, trans. Evan T. Sage, LCL (Cambridge, MA: Harvard University Press, 1935), 421.

8   Savage, *Power through Weakness*, 29.

9   Philostratus, *Apollonius of Tyana*, vol. 2, *Books 5–8*, trans. F. C. Conybeare, LCL (Cambridge, MA: Harvard University Press, 1912), 139.

10 Cicero, *On the Nature of the Gods*, trans. H. Rackham, LCL (Cambridge, MA: Harvard University Press, 1933), 41.

11 Dio Chrysostom, *Discources 1–11*, trans. J. W. Cohoon, LCL (Cambridge, MA: Harvard University Press, 1932), 379; by "others" is meant other Greco-Roman cities.

12 See Bruce Winter, *After Paul Left Corinth: The Influence of Secular Ethics and Social Change* (Grand Rapids, MI: Eerdmans, 2001), 276–86.

reinforcing.[13] The glory of athletic superiority at the games can hardly be overstated. Winners were carried about on shoulders, thrown ribbons, verbally praised with shouts of acclamation, and held in a superlative place of honor. Lucian startles even our modern Western athletic adulation when he comments that the athletes are brought out and paraded naked before the spectators, describing the zeal a typical athlete possesses for his own glory.[14]

Fourth, the Corinthians pursued to excess impressive speech. In terms of the academic world of the time, skill in the spoken word was the noblest aspiration.[15] The value of ancient rhetoric is well-known, and Paul himself lived in the midst of a revival of the importance of classical oratorical skills. This was heightened, however, in Corinth, which appears to have been somewhat different in this regard from Athens, which enjoyed the refined cultivation of the finer art of rhetoric. Corinth, rather, was home to those who sought simply to impress themselves on their audience with as much force as possible. Dio Chrysostom provides a telling example. An eyewitness of the games, he informs us in his "Concerning Virtue" that athletic contests were not the only sphere of competitive self-promotion at the games. He records that "one could hear crowds of wretched sophists around Poseidon's temple shouting and reviling one another, and their disciples, as they were called, fighting with one another, many writers reading aloud their stupid works, many poets reciting their poems while others applauded them."[16]

Fifth and finally, the reputation for sexual immorality earned by ancient Corinth is well-known. The city's temple to the goddess of love, Aphrodite, was reputed to have one thousand cult prostitutes.[17] Whether

13   Oscar Broneer, "The Apostle Paul and the Isthmian Games," *Biblical Archaeologist* 25, no. 1 (1962): 5.

14   Lucian, *Athletics,* trans. A. M. Harmon, in vol. 4 of *The Works of Lucian,* LCL (Cambridge, MA: Harvard University Press, 1925), 61; similarly Savage, *Power through Weakness,* 45.

15   Everett Ferguson, *Backgrounds of Early Christianity,* 3rd ed. (Grand Rapids, MI: Eerdmans, 2003), 111.

16   Dio Chrysostom, *Discources 1–11,* 381. The Isthmian games were dedicated to Poseidon.

17   See Ralph P. Martin's discussion in *2 Corinthians,* WBC (Waco: Word, 1986), xxvii–xxix.

the existence of one thousand temple prostitutes represents an exaggeration or not, other evidence suggests that Corinth was still in a class by itself with respect to sexual immorality. It is now well documented that "to corinthianize" (*korinthiazesthai*), coined by Aristophanes (c. 450–385 BC), meant to fornicate.[18] It is in this category of sexuality that one might also place references to the external beauty coveted in Corinth. Pseudo-Lucian, for example, records his visit to the city of Rhodes, in which he met a certain "Charicles," whom he describes as "a young man from Corinth who is not only handsome but shows some evidence of skillful use of cosmetics, because, I imagine, he wishes to attract the women."[19]

The Corinthian Correspondence against the Backdrop of Corinth

What is so striking as we turn from the first-century secular ethos of Corinth to the Corinthian correspondence is that we see all five of these areas of excess addressed by Paul. I include 1 Corinthians, but I recognize that after the first four chapters of 1 Corinthians, Paul turns to answer various questions the Corinthians have put to him. In 2 Corinthians, Paul is setting the agenda, and the theme of strength through weakness accordingly permeates the entire letter as he seeks to undermine the Corinthians' fleshliness that is infiltrating the church through the super-apostles. Indeed, one way to understand the super-apostles is simply that they were thoroughly Corinthian in mindset but using that mindset within the church. Instead of athletic power and money, they lauded impressive preaching and ministry—the same mindset, just channeled differently.

First, we see money at play in the class distinctions that Paul engages right from the start of the Corinthian correspondence as he reminds his readers that "not many of you were wise according to worldly standards, not many were powerful, not many were of noble birth"

---

18 For an investigation into the development of this, see Murphy-O'Connor, *St. Paul's Corinth*, 56. See also Winter, *After Paul Left Corinth*, 87.

19 Lucian, *Amores*, trans. M. D. Macleod, in vol. 8 of *The Works of Lucian*, LCL (Cambridge, MA: Harvard University Press, 1967), 163.

(1 Cor. 1:26). Material or financial concerns appear a few more times in 1 Corinthians (1 Cor. 6:7; 9:11, 14; 16:1–3). Moving to 2 Corinthians, one finds in chapters 8–9 perhaps the most famous passage on financial generosity in the New Testament. Here (as we have already seen above in chapter 5 on friendship) we find extensive instruction as Paul feels compelled to urge the Corinthians to contribute to the needs of the saints in Jerusalem, particularly in light of the lavish generosity of the much poorer Macedonians (2 Cor. 8:1–5).

With regard to power, second, Paul insists throughout the opening chapters of 1 Corinthians that the gospel may look foolish to the world but in reality "it is the *power* of God" (1 Cor. 1:18; cf. 1 Cor. 1:24; 2:1–5; 13:2). And in 2 Corinthians, Paul assures believers that they do indeed have a treasure, yet it is a treasure contained in a fragile jar of clay. And why should such a bland vessel possess such a precious treasure? The reason is "to show that the surpassing *power* belongs to God and not to us" (2 Cor. 4:7). Hence, even "in afflictions, hardships, calamities," and so on, there is manifested "the power of God" (2 Cor. 6:4, 7). The theme of power is also heavy in 2 Corinthians 10–13, in which Paul argues that "the weapons of our warfare are not of the flesh but have divine power to destroy strongholds" (2 Cor. 10:4), since "the power of Christ" is found where one least expects it: in "weaknesses, insults, hardships, persecutions, and calamities" (2 Cor. 12:9–10). All this is rooted in Christ, who, despite being crucified, now "lives by the power of God" (2 Cor. 13:4).[20] Religious power was an especially coveted element of personal spirituality in Corinthian Christianity.[21]

Third, athleticism is also present, as we find references to the athletic games in the Corinthian correspondence, most prominently in 1 Corinthians 9 as Paul exhorts believers to run the race with zeal

---

20 P. J. Gräbe, "The All-Surpassing Power of God through the Holy Spirit in the Midst of Our Broken Earthly Existence: Perspectives on Paul's Use of *dunamis* in 2 Corinthians," *Neot* 28, no. 1 (1994): 147–56, examines exegetically the three central pericopes in which Paul speaks of power in 2 Corinthians: 4:7; 6:7; 12:9.

21 The various forms of the Greek root for power (*dunamis*) occur forty-nine times in 1–2 Corinthians, more than any other Pauline letter by far.

and to discipline themselves the way athletes do (1 Cor. 9:24–27). In 2 Corinthians 4:9, the reference to being "struck down" may be a reference to Olympic wrestling,[22] and Paul's quote of his opponents in 2 Corinthians 10:10, accusing him of being weak in bodily presence, though not necessarily an athletic reference, coalesces with the kind of bodily vanity fueled by the games, as noted above, since it refers to Paul's diminutive physical stature.

Fourth, regarding rhetoric and the spoken word, both Corinthian letters are replete with this theme. Throughout 1 Corinthians, Paul repeatedly expresses his resistance to rhetorical eloquence lest the gospel's power and clarity be minimized (1 Cor. 1:17; 2:1–5; 4:19; 13:1). We find similar references to humanly wise speech versus authentically divine speech in 2 Corinthians, especially the final four chapters, in which Paul's opponents are most conspicuously in view. He goes so far as to cite the accusation of those undermining his apostolic authority in 2 Corinthians 10:10: "For they say, 'His letters are weighty and strong, but his bodily presence is weak, and his speech of no account.'" Paul freely admits that he is "unskilled in speaking" (2 Cor. 11:6), yet that is not problematic in the economy of the paradoxical gospel; indeed "it is in the sight of God that we have been speaking" (2 Cor. 12:19). Not only the style of Paul's speech but the content, too, was less than agreeable to the Corinthians. Paul also explicitly rejected the self-promoting motivation that fueled some Corinthian speaking and caused comparing among men (2 Cor. 10:12).

Fifth and finally, excess in the realm of sexuality can be detected in the Corinthian correspondence. It confronts us startlingly in 1 Corinthians 5 with Paul's instructions regarding a man fornicating with his father's wife and the Corinthians' lack of dismay (1 Cor. 5:2). The "sexually immoral" top the list of "the unrighteous" in 1 Corinthians 6:9–10, at the end of which Paul explicitly claims, "Such were some of you" (1 Cor. 6:11). He returns at length to sexual purity in the second half of the chapter (1 Cor. 6:12–20) and then commences immediately

22 So C. Spicq, "L'Image sportive de 2 Corinthiens 4,7–9," *ETL* 13 (1937): 202–29.

with a discussion of marriage (1 Cor. 7:1–16) that, though no longer directly addressing sexual immorality, does not entirely leave the issue behind (1 Cor. 7:5, 9). Paul again warns against sexual immorality in 1 Corinthians 10:8. This issue is not as pervasive in 2 Corinthians, though Paul may have it in mind as he instructs the Corinthians not to be "unequally yoked with unbelievers" in 2 Corinthians 6:14–7:1. The call to "cleanse ourselves from every defilement of body and spirit" (2 Cor. 7:1) while perhaps more inclusive than merely sexual defilement, certainly cannot refer to less than this.[23]

When we consider these observations from 1–2 Corinthians together with the social picture painted by extrabiblical sources, a compelling case presents itself that these five points of excess were indeed problematic in the church at Corinth. These five elements, moreover, are not disparate, unrelated problems but five interconnected fruits of the single root of Corinthian excess. We have seen, then, that the Corinthian culture fed off excess in a variety of manifestations. And we have seen that the Corinthian correspondence is manifestly cognizant of these problems of excess. What we have not yet seen is how Paul addresses these problems.

Strength through Weakness in 2 Corinthians

To this point I have allowed five particular areas of worldly pursuit to determine our reflections. Now that we have a clear grasp of Corinthian society and have also seen that Paul reflects an awareness of all five of these in the two canonical letters to the church there, we are set up to look at 2 Corinthians in particular. What we find is a pervasive motif of paradoxical upending of the fleshly mindset that had apparently infected the church at Corinth and was being nurtured by the super-apostles. As Paul speaks time and again in 2 Corinthians of life through death, comfort through pain, and strength through weakness, he is going to the root of Corinthian worldliness and lancing it

---

23 Barnett suggests that sexual sin is on Paul's mind in 2 Cor. 12:20–13:4 too. Paul Barnett, *The Second Epistle to the Corinthians*, NICNT (Grand Rapids, MI: Eerdmans, 1997), 606.

with the paradoxes of the gospel. I have used the theme of "strength through weakness" as the title of this chapter, but this is just one of the ways that Paul upends Corinthian fleshliness with the basic motif of paradox or the upside-down nature of the way God works in the world and supremely in the gospel.

I cannot do an exhaustive survey of this theme, partly because it is so prevalent (and partly because I have a word-count limit to obey for this book). The below chart offers one way to get a macro-perspective of the counterintuitive motif running through the letter. We will pick up on just ten of the clearest examples of this motif to bring out how pervasive this recurring paradoxical twist is, but many more could be identified and explored.[24]

Outline of 2 Corinthians as Seen through the Upside-Down Nature of the Gospel

Text	Paradox			Encapsulated in
I. The Apostle: Gospel Ministry Explained (2 Cor. 1–7)				
1:1–2	(Greeting)			
1:3–7	Comfort	through	affliction	(1:5–6)
1:8–11	Confidence	through	despair	(1:9)
1:12–22	Grace	through	simplicity	(1:12, 15)
1:23–2:4	Joy	through	pain	(2:3)
2:5–11	(Reconciliation for the Sinner)			
2:12–17	Victory	through	captivity	(2:14)
3:1–6	Sufficiency	through	insufficiency	(3:5)
3:7–11	(A Greater Glory [argumentum a fortiori])			
3:12–18	Transformation	through	unveiling	(3:12–13)
4:1–6	Ministry	through	self-renunciation	(4:5)
4:7–15	Life	through	death	(4:11)
4:16–18	Renewal	through	corrosion	(4:16)

24 A comprehensive exploration of this theme of strength through weakness can be found in Dane C. Ortlund, "Less Is More: Paul's Theology of Paradox in 2 Corinthians" (ThM thesis, Covenant Theological Seminary, 2007).

Text	Paradox			Encapsulated in
5:1–10	Dwelling	through	homelessness	(5:1)
5:11–21	Sinlessness	through	sinfulness	(5:21)
6:1–13	Blessing	through	suffering	(6:10)
6:14–7:1	Welcoming	through	separation	(6:17–18)
7:2–16	Joy	through	affliction	(7:10)

II. The Audience: Generous Moneyhandling Exhorted (2 Cor. 8–9)

8:1–24	Abundance	through	poverty	(8:9, 14)
9:1–15	Reaping	through	giving	(9:6)

III. The Agitators: Gain-Seeking Measurement Exposed (2 Cor. 10–13)

10:1–18	Commendation	through	denigration	(10:10, 18)
11:1–15	Exaltation	through	humbling	(11:7)
11:16–33	Confidence	through	hardship	(11:30)
12:1–10	Strength	through	weakness	(12:9–10)
12:11–21	Superiority	through	inferiority	(12:11, 15)
13:1–4	Power	through	weakness	(13:4)
13:5–10	Approval	through	apparent disapproval	(13:7, 9)
13:11–14	(Closing)			

Comfort through Affliction (1:5–7)

In words appropriate to the start of an epistle that returns repeatedly to the theme of unanticipated blessings through (not despite) suffering, Paul connects the suffering and attendant comfort of both the Corinthians and his own ministry (with Timothy).[25] The noteworthy point for our purposes is that Paul does not simply address suffering and comfort and observe that both presently occur (whether in his own ministry or in the experience of the Corinthians). Rather, the two are inextricably linked and, in the economy of the gospel, mutually reinforcing. Christian comfort, says Paul, flows smoothest along

---

25 Various forms of the noun *paraklēsis* (comfort, exhortation, consolation) and the verb *parakaleō* (to comfort, exhort, console) occur ten times in 2 Cor. 1:3–7; forms of the noun *thlipsis* (affliction, tribulation), the verb *thlibō* (to afflict, trouble), the noun *pathēma* (sufferings), and the verb *paschō* (to suffer) occur a total of eight times in 1:3–11.

the avenue of suffering. Though one would expect misery to abound where sufferings abound and expect comfort to abound where stability abounds, Paul claims just the opposite. "For just as we share abundantly in the sufferings of Christ," says Paul, "so also our comfort abounds through Christ" (2 Cor. 1:5 NIV). Paul employs the familiar "just as . . . so also . . ." formula to bring out the distinct yet indivisible pairing of suffering and comfort.

Paul then explains that this comfort is not intended solely for personal relief but is meant to spill out in human relationship, suggesting in 1:6 that whatever happens to him, the goal is the Corinthians' spiritual welfare. He then concludes by returning to the truth first mentioned in 1:5, explaining that he has solid hopes for the Corinthians as a result of their fellow participation in his sufferings-unto-comfort. In 1:7, however, Paul applies this paradoxical principle not to his own ministry (as in 1:5) but to the experience of the Corinthians. The Corinthians' sufferings consolidate their association with both Paul (a point they reluctantly conceded) and Christ (a point they readily conceded).

It is also important to note that right from the start both suffering and comfort are rooted in Christ: Christ is the model and the source of both. This thought will surface again in 5:12–21, in chapters 8–9, and at the closing of the epistle, where the experience of Christ himself is couched in terms of paradox: "He was crucified in weakness, but lives by the power of God" (13:4).[26]

In this opening section to the epistle, then, Paul sets the tone for a reading in which paradox is the hermeneutical key to unlocking the letter.

Confidence through Despair (1:8–9)

Continuing on his autobiographical tour of his own sufferings along with Timothy, Paul goes so far as to say that they felt so burdened that they did not even expect to live through the trial—thus they had in

---

26 Elegantly expressed in Richard Bauckham, "Weakness—Paul's and Ours," *Them* 7, no. 3 (1982): 5.

themselves a sentence of death. Indeed, it was an "excess" (*hyperbolē*, 1:8[27]) of difficulty beyond any innate human ability to cope. Yet the reason Paul brings this up is neither to solely provide information nor to curry empathy but to explain the purpose of it. And that express purpose is so that they might have confidence in God.

For Paul, despair ultimately was the doorway to confidence, for it casts him on God. This counterintuitive sentiment would, it seems, have caught the Corinthians quite off guard. And again Paul roots this paradox in the experience of Christ, though implicitly, when he refers to the "God who raises the dead" (1:9).

Sufficiency through Insufficiency (3:1–6)

The principial upside-down nature of the gospel that permeates 2 Corinthians pivots in a new direction in this passage in that, unlike the world, Paul does not build himself up as a means of defending the legitimacy of his ministerial fatherhood of the Corinthians. He is not a self-promoter. Rather, the Corinthians themselves are Paul's credentials. The absence of self-promotion is possible because of the presence of living letters. The Spirit is greater than the tablets. Counterintuitively, the invisible trumps the visible. As a result, Paul says that his confidence before God finds its origin in God and in God alone (3:5).

We have already explored the eschatological significance of these six verses in earlier chapters. Now we simply observe the startling combination of both insufficiency and sufficiency (*hikano-* prefix cognates, three times in 3:5–6). Such personal insufficiency is the occasion, through Christ, for confidence. Participants in the new covenant have no sufficiency in themselves, but because of this—and only when it is recognized—they participate in the very Spirit of God and the new realm sufficiency that comes with it. Recognition

---

27 This is a particularly significant word in 2 Corinthians. We have already drawn attention to the fact that the Corinthians were obsessed with excess; in light of this observation I am intrigued to note more occurrences of this noun and its cognates (the verb *hyperballō* and the adverb *hyperballontōs*) in 2 Corinthians than any other New Testament book (eight of the fourteen New Testament occurrences: 2 Cor. 1:8; 3:10; 4:7, 17 [2x]; 9:14; 11:23; 12:7).

of one's insufficiency is, when brought to Christ, the acquisition of true sufficiency.

Because this sufficiency is rooted in Christ and not self, Paul's thinking is set off sharply from Stoic and Cynic thought current at the time. Stoicism, for example, was no stranger to the kinds of lists of hardships Paul presents in 6:3–11 and 11:22–30. What makes Paul so different from such philosophers, however, is that the locus of strength for overcoming such difficulties lies in divine sufficiency, not self-sufficiency. Stoics looked inward for the resources to calmly ignore and endure the calamities of life.[28] Paul looked outside himself. Hence from this perspective, Paul and the Stoics are operating on polar opposite frameworks when it comes to undergoing suffering. Our sufficiency, says the apostle, is from God.

Life through Death (4:7–12)

In 4:6 Paul describes the inner treasure of regeneration, in which one comes to be illumined by "the light of the knowledge of the glory of God in the face of Jesus Christ." Having described this inner reality in 3:1–4:6, he now moves to the outer casing in which such reality exists: frail human bodies, particularly those whose frailty is exacerbated by suffering. "But we have this treasure [described in preceding verses] in jars of clay, to show that the surpassing power belongs to God and not to us" (4:7). Paul is exposing the strong disjunction between the internal glory, written on tablets of human hearts, wrought not by the letter but by the Spirit, in which the glory of God shines in our hearts, on the one hand, and the *vehicle* of such glory on the other.

What is God's purpose in using such frailty? It was for the demonstration of divine (not human) power—a theme similar to the human insufficiency / divine sufficiency theme of chapter 3, as well as 1:9, in which the sentence of death Paul felt was in order to manifest God as the one to be relied on. The human impulse to assert oneself in one's own strength, which we have seen to be uniquely strong in Corinthian

---

28   See Troels Engberg-Pedersen, *Paul and the Stoics* (Edinburgh: T&T Clark, 2000), 45–79.

culture, is again flipped upside down. The display of God's power is achieved by human bodily frailty.

That human corporeality is the referent of "jars of clay" is evidenced by what follows in 4:10–12. In a sentence in which he repeatedly lifts up the opposites of life and death, Paul writes that we appropriate Jesus's physical death in our own "mortal flesh" for the purpose of the manifestation of Jesus's life. This is critical: there is a direct causal connection between the human experience of "death" and the manifestation of divine life. Paul's point, in other words, is not merely that both can coexist, but that one indeed leads to the other. To put it most strongly, it is impossible to experience the life of Jesus without experiencing the death of Jesus. Paul seems to be saying that just as Jesus died to impart life, so there is a similar pattern in apostolic ministry: Paul too "dies" to impart (Jesus's) life (cf. Gal. 2:20; Phil. 3:10). Hence 2 Corinthians 4:12, which moves from Paul and Jesus to Paul and the Corinthians: "So death is at work in us, but life in you."

A Christian is a paradox: a treasure is active inside, even as the outer reality screams the contrary, and the latter is the means to the former. Daily death is not that which must be avoided to gain life. It is inextricably tied up with—and even, in a strange way, the pathway to—life. C. K. Barrett argues and John Calvin suggests that Paul is speaking mainly of the future resurrection here.[29] Yet 4:10–11 indicate that it is not only a present death but also a present life that is manifested. It is only in 4:17–18 and into chapter 5 that Paul steps back and considers the consummate eschatological raising to life. Yet while the future resurrection is not in the foreground in 4:10–12, neither is it wholly lost from view. For the present life, believers' experience, even in the midst of (and because of) the death(s) they experience, is a taste now of what is to come in fullness in the eschaton when the new realm that dawned with Christ's first coming is completed with his second coming.

---

29 C. K. Barrett, *The Second Epistle to the Corinthians*, BNTC (Peabody, MA: Hendrickson, 1973), 140; John Calvin, *Commentaries on the Epistles of Paul the Apostle to the Corinthians*, vol. 2, trans. John Pringle (Grand Rapids, MI: Baker, 2003), 205.

Blessing through Suffering (6:3–10)

We come to the first of two lists of difficulties (the second in 2 Corinthians 11), comprising two of the clearest statements of paradox in this epistle (cf. 1 Cor. 4:9–13).[30] For both lists manifest the paradox Paul aims to plant in the hearts of the Corinthians that the self-satisfaction they seek is found in the very thing they despise: the humiliation of self-emptying.

The list in 2 Corinthians 6 consists of three groups of nine. The first third lists experiences the Corinthians would have eschewed; the second, conversely, lists traits the Corinthians would have embraced; the third does the unthinkable and (paradoxically) combines these together, ending on the starkest note of paradox with the final triad of 6:10. Paul introduces the list in 6:4 by saying that he and his co-laborers "as servants of God . . . commend ourselves in every way." Paul then proceeds to "commend" himself with the very things that, to their mind, erode apostolic authenticity in 6:4–5:

- endurance[31]
- afflictions
- hardships
- calamities
- beatings
- imprisonments
- riots
- labors
- sleepless nights

At this point Paul's litany of sources of commendation takes a strange twist. He has spoken of the difficulties that commend his ministry, which the Corinthians were evidently quite reticent to associate with

---

30 For a study of the lists of hardships suffered by Paul as outlined in 1 and 2 Corinthians, see John T. Fitzgerald, *Cracks in an Earthen Vessel: An Examination of the Catalogues of Hardships in the Corinthian Correspondence* (Atlanta: Scholars, 1988).

31 While the first item, endurance, would be a virtue in the minds of both Paul and the Corinthians, the kind of situation calling for such endurance, like the next eight items in the list, would indeed grate against the Corinthians' ideal of an apostle.

an apostolic leader of theirs; now (moving from 6:5 to 6:6) he speaks
of those ministerial characteristics with which the Corinthians would,
it appears, very much agree as the signs of a true worker for Christ.
The smoothness with which Paul moves from hardships to traits more
amenable to the Corinthian vision for ministry underlines the seam-
lessness between the two in Paul's (not the Corinthians') mind. The
sufferings and the virtues go hand in hand because the former supply
the soil in which the latter flourish. The Corinthians seem desirous to
extract the virtue while leaving behind the suffering.

Paul continues in 6:5–7:

- hunger
- purity
- knowledge
- patience
- kindness
- the Holy Spirit
- genuine love
- truthful speech
- the power of God

After this middle third, Paul takes another unanticipated turn, listing puzzling couplets that serve as means of his apostolic ministry,
bringing together in startling companionship anti-Corinthian with
pro-Corinthian sentiment: "through honor and dishonor, through
slander and praise. We are treated as imposters, and yet are true;
as unknown, and yet well known; as dying, and behold, we live;
as punished, and yet not killed" (6:8–9). Paul mixes together the
extremes of those things to which the Corinthians quickly latched
on (honor, praise, truth, being well known, living, not being killed)
with those things they fled from (dishonor, slander, being imposters,
being unknown, dying, punishment). One imagines the cringing or
blank stares of the self-respecting Corinthians upon the reading of
the letter in the public assembly.

The reason Paul can combine such opposites and seemingly mutually exclusive realities is found in 6:10, in which Paul continues with three more puzzling pairs. Yet he makes explicit the paradoxes of new realm Christianity: "as sorrowful, yet always rejoicing; as poor, yet making many rich." Unlike the preceding six pairs of 6:8–9, the first two pairs of 6:10 employ *de* as the connecting conjunction, which ought to be taken as an adversative ("but") both because it stands in stark contrast to the preceding instances of *kai* and because what is being connected in 6:10 are, on the surface, opposites. Then comes the climactic pair that serves as an umbrella to all that has come before and elucidates Paul's paradox most clearly—"as having nothing, yet possessing everything." With his reversion back to *kai* as the connecting conjunction, as well as the strongest possible pair of opposites—within which all that has come before in this list can be subsumed—Paul brings the paradoxical nature of his apostolic leadership most clearly into the light.

Paul has squeezed out any possible remaining room for his readers to misunderstand him. He has driven his point home with increasing and finally climactic force: the way up is down. The way to possess is to be dispossessed; the way to enrich many is to be poor; the way to joy is through grief. (Real) joy, (true) riches, and (meaningful) possessions come *through* grief, poverty, and lack, respectively—not in avoidance of these things.

Joy through Affliction (7:4–7)

"*In* all our affliction," the apostle writes, "I am overflowing with joy" (7:4). Here again the paradox surfaces, echoing 1:3–11 as Paul again combines "affliction" (7:4) with "comforts" (7:6), though this time in the context of vindicating the genuineness of his love for the Corinthians (cf. also 2:3–4). The reason Paul gives for this strange conjunction of hard circumstances with newly ignited cheer is his being reunited with Titus, who not only himself comforted Paul but who blessed Paul with the overflowing blessing Titus had received from the Corinthians, despite being the probable carrier of Paul's earlier severe letter (2:1–4).

And Paul writes that this joy has come as one who is afflicted because God comforts the "downcast" (7:6). Though the adjective generally means "humble" in the sense of the Christian virtue opposite prideful, here it has the sense of "humiliatedness."[32] As in 2 Corinthians 1, then, there is a profound comfort that comes only through humiliating affliction, not in the avoidance of it. Hence Paul can declare, "In all our affliction, I am overflowing with joy" (7:4).

Abundance through Poverty (8:1–2)

Moving into a two-chapter section intended to generate financial generosity on behalf of the needy church at Jerusalem, we see Paul apply his disruptive, counterintuitive framework, so needed by the Corinthians, to the realm of money.

Beginning with the example of the Macedonians, Paul points out in 8:2 that the generous Macedonians experienced an "abundance of joy" in the midst of "a severe test of affliction." The verse is loaded with the language of stark contrast: affliction and joy, poverty and wealth. Again, we find the coveted state of joy, not despite suffering, but in its midst. Yet instead of describing the positive result as comfort (as in 1:3–11 and 7:4–11), Paul speaks of the Macedonians' *joy*. The clause "in a severe test of affliction," fronted in 8:2, is not at all necessary if Paul simply wants to set forth the exemplary generosity of the Macedonians. All that is necessary to speak of the Macedonians' generosity is their giving in spite of their poverty, but Paul goes beyond merely describing the Macedonian financial situation. He also points to the affliction they were experiencing, whether this was connected with their poverty or independent of it. That is, Paul draws attention to the fact that the Macedonians not only experienced a wealth of generosity in the midst of poverty but also an abundance of joy in the midst of affliction.

This observation, viewed in light of Corinthian sensibilities, as well as the rest of this epistle, suggests that here too Paul is not only en-

---

32 Barrett, *Second Corinthians*, 207. For this usage by Paul of the word and its cognates, see Rom. 12:16; Phil. 3:21.

couraging the Corinthians to obey (this time, with their finances) but also portraying the truth that radical, self-denying obedience contains within it a paradoxical blessing that far outweighs the loss incurred.

Confidence through Hardship (11:21–33)

As we come to Paul's lengthy list of hardships in 2 Corinthians 11, we are confronted with one of the strongest instances of Paul's strategy of exposing Corinthian worldliness by affirming his own apostolic integrity *by virtue of his suffering*.

The point to which I wish to draw attention, then, is that Paul begins his list by referring to it as a list of boasting (11:16, 18) and ends his list the very same way (11:30; 12:1). Yet such a label appears on first glance to be startlingly inappropriate since, bracketed out by itself, 11:22–29 hardly contains items worthy of parading before others. Indeed, while the list initially sounds simply like the pouting of a somber misanthrope, when one realizes that this is not a concession of unfortunate events so much as a resumé recounting reasons for self-confidence, they sound more like the ravings of a deranged masochist.

The apostle begins his list with a few items for which the Corinthians would have contentedly nodded their approval—he is a Hebrew, an Israelite, the offspring of Abraham, a servant of Christ. Cheers all around. Yet at this point Paul's litany of qualifications makes a 180-degree turn as Paul defines just *how* he is a servant of Christ. He speaks of the extreme difficulties he has undergone, leaving no sphere of circumstance untouched—human persecution, natural disaster, exposure to the elements, and emotional storms are all included.

What purpose, then, does such a list serve? Why does Paul promote the very things that appear to detract from, rather than affirm, his apostolic authenticity? The key is 11:30: "If I must boast"—Paul is reluctant to do so (cf. 12:1)—"I will boast of the things that show my weakness." Paul plays to the Corinthian method while subverting the substance of that method. That is, Paul does not scold the Corinthians' silly boasting as the immature self-absorption of children, calling them instead to a more mature humility. To do so may have actually exacerbated the delicate error he was trying to untangle by instead giving the Corinthians (had they succeeded in leaving behind such childish pridefulness) one more thing in which to boast. They might have persisted, in other words, in comparing themselves with one another (10:12)—this time with reference to their relative modesty.

Rather Paul beats them at their own game, ironically exulting in the very things the super-apostles would eschew. Yet while employing the same method (boasting), Paul penetrates to the root of the Corinthian mindset by exposing the essence of their mistake. He subverts the content of one's boasting. Paul boasts all right—*of his weakness.* To a church clamoring for superiority among themselves, this not only cut off the weeds visible above the surface but exposed the root underground.

As a final autobiographical detail to cap his own strength through weakness, Paul speaks of his being lowered in a basket through a window in order to escape the watching eye of the governor while in Damascus (11:32–33). Though at first this detail seems anticlimactic at best and a redactic interpolation at worst, it is in fact the pinnacle of Paul's litany of weaknesses. This is all the clearer when seen against the pervasive epistolary backdrop of paradox that this chapter has been seeking to demonstrate. For while in these two verses Paul speaks of how he was *lowered,* in the next several verses (12:1–6) he describes how he was *raised* (to "the third heaven"). As the imposed literary break between chapter 11 and chapter 12 melts away, then, one sees once more the paradox so thoroughly informing Paul's theological rhetoric in 2 Corinthians.

Strength through Weakness (12:1–10)

To the readers of 2 Corinthians, the opening verses of chapter 12 may sound as if Paul has finally gotten his head screwed on straight. At last, after a litany of hardships in which the apostle finds some strange satisfaction, he relates a *truly* boast-worthy experience. Paul himself was evidently caught up into the heavenly world and given a glimpse of divine resplendence that no known words can adequately describe

(12:1–6), which we explored in the previous chapter. This he now describes to the glory-hungry Corinthians.

Yet as soon as these hopes for a more sensible measurement of apostolic legitimacy are raised, they are dashed. For Paul relays this inexpressible experience only as prolegomenon to an attendant difficulty: a "thorn in the flesh." We today might picture a small rosebush thorn, but the term used (*skolops*) could designate objects as large as a stake on which one was impaled. The thorn generated more than mere annoyance; it generated agony corresponding to the glory of what Paul had seen in the highest heaven. Though the thorn was (presumably) introduced into Paul's life fourteen years prior, 12:8–10 give every indication that it is a present reality still and thus represents a prolonged, sustained pain. But what was the thorn? Speculation does us no good. We do not know. And that is just as well, lest those whose afflictions are of a different nature than Paul's feel unable to apply his teaching to their own experiences. Probably Paul is intentionally vague, not only for maximal application but also to prevent spotlighting his own life any more than necessary. Paul's point is not the content of the thorn but its intent.[33]

And what is that intent? Paul's humility: "to keep me from becoming conceited" (12:7). The verb (*hyperairomai*) means to be lifted up. The thorn's purpose is to deflate the certainty that Paul would quietly become puffed up over his indescribable experience of heaven. And who wouldn't, without a thorn to burst that bubble? And so the Lord lovingly, gently, sovereignly afflicts his dear apostle. Or did he? Doesn't the text ascribe the thorn to Satan or one of his emissaries? Indeed. The thorn was given to "harass" Paul—surely the work of the devil. Yet surrounding this desire to harass is a purpose to humble Paul, mentioned twice, once at the beginning of 12:7 and once at the end. The sandwiching of Satan's purpose within God's reflects the greater reality: the sandwiching of Satan's work and power within God's. In a mysterious overlay of

---

33 This paragraph and the next several are adapted from Dane Ortlund, *2 Corinthians*, in *Romans–Galatians*, vol. 10 of *ESV Expository Commentary* (Wheaton, IL: Crossway, 2020), 547–50. Used by permission.

divine sovereignty and evil, even satanic activity falls within the scope of God's sovereign purposes. God is not the author of evil in such a way that renders him morally culpable. He is incapable of doing anything that is morally tainted. Yet even the most evil act of human history was ordained by God (Acts 2:23; 4:28). So too with lesser evils.

So Paul does in 2 Corinthians 12:8 what any of us would do. He asks for the thorn to be removed. Just as the "third" heaven likely refers to the heaven of heavens, the heart of heaven, so "three times" likely means Paul pleaded with the Lord to exhaustion. He didn't make the request more than twice but fewer than four times; rather, it was a complete, comprehensive, full request. He did not ask timidly or passingly. The very verb he uses, "I pleaded" (using *parakaleō*), not simply "I asked," already makes this clear. That Paul pleads with the Lord to have the thorn removed is further proof that the Lord is the one providentially behind the giving of the thorn.

Paul saw two ways forward. The Lord could (1) remove the thorn, and Paul could get on with life and ministry; or (2) leave the thorn, and Paul would be forever crippled and slowed in life and ministry. The Lord responded with yet a third option: leave the thorn, but give Paul grace (12:9). And the net result for Paul's life and ministry would be to accomplish by divine power what he could never have attained otherwise. This is God's secret strategy for his people. This is the surprising way into power from on high.

God's "grace" in 12:9 is not primarily objective, forgiving grace (as in, say, Rom. 3:24). Rather, Paul is using "grace" more broadly as shorthand for the presence of God—sustaining, empowering, calming, supporting, comforting, emboldening, satisfying. "My grace is sufficient for you" means "*I* am sufficient for you." Why then use the word "grace"? Because the Lord wants to reassure Paul that he need not earn or deserve God's presence. It is of grace. This grace is further clarified by the next clause: "for my power is made perfect in weakness." This grace channels divine *power*. The presence of God will sustain Paul; the power of God will strengthen him. What we must not miss is that it is not Paul's strength but God's. Paul's contribution is weakness. But this is not a concession; it is precisely what God delights to work with. This is the mystery, the wonder, the glory, of new realm Christianity united to a crucified Lord: our weakness attracts, not repels, God's own power. Our lowness and incapacities, which we naturally fear and flee, is precisely where God loves to dwell.

As a result, Paul's pursuits are flipped upside down. He had been given a revelation of heaven in 12:1–6, but he has been given a revelation of how heaven intersects with fallen sinners in 12:7–10—namely, through human weakness. The first revelation brought him way up high; the second, way down low (perhaps Paul had his heavenly vision and his thorn in the flesh in mind when he said in Romans 8 that neither "height nor depth" can "separate us from the love of God in Christ" [Rom. 8:39]). And this second revelation has inverted his source of boasting. Instead of building his identity on his areas of strength, he builds his identity on the very weakness the world and the flesh abjure. Competence is not where God's power lies. Frailty is. Feebleness. For there, God's grace ignites. There God himself dwells. Indeed, Paul uses ancient language to speak of God's power resting upon him (2 Cor. 12:9). The verb for "rest" (*episkēnoō*) is built on the root word for tabernacle, the portable temple in which alone God's presence dwelt in times of old. But while God's power was once cordoned off from all weak and defiled sinners, now it is precisely the weakness of sinners that draws in the power of God. Once more we see Paul quietly indicating that the new age has dawned in Christ. And in this new age, God's power does not operate the way we expect.

In 12:10 Paul comes to the triumphant conclusion of his thorn experience. This is also probably the high point of the entire letter. This verse crystallizes and illumines Paul's entire argument in 2 Corinthians, concluding the strength through weakness theme that we are seeing throughout the epistle.

Having seen now the secret to the power of Christ tabernacling upon him, Paul fills out what he means in 12:9 by "I will boast all the more gladly of my weaknesses." What kind of weaknesses? Paul answers with a list of five categories of increasing intensity of difficulty:

"weaknesses" (the general, summarizing category, denoting all fallen human incapacities), "insults" (mistreatment by others), "hardships" (experiences that squeeze Paul, forcing him to uncomfortable limits), "persecutions" (afflictions at the hands of hostile enemies), and "calamities" (truly overwhelming experiences, devastating circumstances). Paul says that he is "content with" (*eudokeō*) these things, but the Greek verb is stronger than that. It means to "be well pleased with" or to "delight in" something—used, for example, of the Father being "well pleased" with the Son in Matthew 3:17. Paul is not saying that he is merely "content" with all these things that render him frail and weak. He steps into them. He embraces them. This is a tone not of resignation but of eagerness. To be clear, this is no masochism; he does not delight in the weaknesses for themselves. This is clarified by his addition of "for the sake of Christ." Paul delights in weakness because it opens him up to heaven's blessings and strength. His spiritual power surges forward.

And so, to sum up: "For when I am weak, then I am strong" (2 Cor. 12:10). Paul is not referring simply to isolated and occasional experiences of weakness in which case strength ignites. The Greek word rendered "when" suggests that he has in mind a perpetual state of weakness, and thus a perpetual state of receiving divine strength. Paul saw now that his weakness was not an obstacle to, but the gateway into, God's strength.

Power through Weakness (13:3–4)

Here at the close of the letter, Paul brings the Corinthians back to the foundation from which all paradoxical language describing Christianity has sprung: the life, death, and resurrection of Christ himself. In one of the clearest expressions of paradox in the epistle, Paul explains that Christ is not, as he appeared outwardly to those who killed him, weak. He is powerful.

The logic in 13:4 is as follows:

- Christ was weak at one time; indeed, he was crucified.
- Yet he is now powerful, due to living by the power of God.

- Similarly, we are weak—both in ourselves and through our union with this one who was crucified.
- Yet this same weakness that unites us to his weakness unites us also to his power.

With Christ, the paradigm setter, power came through weakness, not in the avoidance of it. So it is with his followers.

Everything in this chapter thus far is true, so far as it goes, yet remains unconsummated or locked without the Christological key. For Christ is the ultimate example of someone who experienced weakness yet was made strong through this weakness (Phil. 2:6–11). In three critical ways—one of degree, one of example, and one of vicariousness—Christ consummates the biblical-theological theme of strength through weakness.[34]

First, Christ experienced both weakness and strength to a superlative degree. On the one hand, it is impossible to fathom the profound weakness to which God the Son was subjected. It is popular in American evangelical teaching to depict Jesus as possessing all the characteristics and powers of deity at the snap of his fingers, as evidenced in his miracles and supernatural knowledge. This fails, however, to grapple fully with Jesus's utter humanity. And Christ's weakness plummeted to its lowest depths in the gruesome shame of the cross. Conversely, the exaltation of Christ to God's right hand portrays a "strength" of status and glory as high in degree as his humiliation was low.[35] Let us frame the point, once more, in biblical-theological terms. Certainly Jews were aware of the theme of a lowly suffering servant from Isaiah 40–55. What would have been shocking was to overlay this role with that of the glorious son of man of Daniel 7 and the Davidic king of 2 Samuel 7 (along with a handful of messianic psalms). The weakness

---

34 This paragraph and the next few are adapted from Dane C. Ortlund, "'Power Is Made Perfect in Weakness' (2 Cor. 12:9): A Biblical Theology of Strength through Weakness," *Presbyterion* 36, no. 2 (2010): 86–108. Used by permission.

35 See Richard Bauckham, *Jesus and the God of Israel: God Crucified and Other Studies on the New Testament's Christology of Divine Identity* (Grand Rapids, MI: Eerdmans, 2008), 197–210.

of the suffering servant and the strength of the son of man and son of David intersected in a single individual.[36]

Christ's weakness and strength are not to be coolly appreciated from a distance, however, but emulated, for while Christ is in a class by himself in the *degree* of his weakness and strength, Christians do follow him in *kind*. This brings us to the second way in which Christ embodies the climactic paradox of strength through weakness. Jesus not only bore a cross but instructed his followers to take up their cross and follow him, in what Michael Gorman has recently reiterated as "cruciformity" or "cruciform power," since it is rooted in Christ's own experience of power in weakness.[37] Jesus displayed strength through weakness; so, according to the New Testament, ought we. Christ is not only the *climactic* example of strength through weakness but also the *paradigmatic* example. Believers are united to Christ in both (the weakness of) his death and (the strength of) his resurrection.

Even here, however, we have not yet penetrated to the core insight regarding Christological strength through weakness. We have said that Christ was superlatively weak and superlatively strong, and we have connected that weakness and strength to Christian discipleship. What we have not yet uncovered is the fundamental *resource* by which Christians are to experience strength through weakness. For not only are believers to imitate Christ's weakness and strength but also, in the great exchange, Christ's strength has become ours, and our weakness has become his. Martin Luther in his own time called this the "joyous exchange," and Morna Hooker in our time describes this as the Pauline notion of "interchange"—a notion found most clearly articulated

---

36 See Hans K. LaRondelle, *The Israel of God in Prophecy: Principles of Prophetic Interpretation* (Berrien Springs, MI: Andrews University Press, 1983), 95; Herman N. Ridderbos, *Paul and Jesus: Origin and Character of Paul's Preaching of Christ*, trans. David H. Freedman (Nutley, NJ: Presbyterian & Reformed, 1977), 29–33.

37 Michael J. Gorman, *Inhabiting the Cruciform God: Kenosis, Justification, and Theosis in Paul's Narrative Soteriology* (Grand Rapids, MI: Eerdmans, 2009), 25–34, 121–23; cf. Michael J. Gorman, *Cruciformity: Paul's Narrative Spirituality of the Cross* (Grand Rapids, MI: Eerdmans, 2001), 268–303.

in none other than 2 Corinthians (e.g., 5:21; 8:9).[38] We go down in order to go up, as Christ did; yet in the most ultimate sense, he went down so that we need not. Christ's weakness executed the salvation of weak people.

Strength through Weakness and the New Realm

As this chapter and this book draw to a close, we return to the overarching theme we have been pursuing, that of inaugurated eschatology. How does the theme of strength through weakness fit with the new realm?

One way to express it would be: the new realm is the country through which we are traveling, while strength through weakness is the path that moves us along. Inaugurated eschatology is the "where"; strength through weakness the "how."

This is not to say that in Old Testament times God functioned in a different way than he does now. Time and again, we see God choose the weak and the obscure to accomplish his redemptive purposes. It is weak-tongued Moses, insecure Gideon, and timid Jeremiah who are called by Yahweh to do great deeds and lead God's people. Time and again the ancient law of primogeniture is overturned, and the younger son is chosen rather than the older son.[39]

Yet in the New Testament the theme of strength through weakness explodes into full flower with the first coming of Christ. He came in weakness and ignominy and was even crucified at the end of his earthly ministry. Even in his earthly teaching, we saw him preparing his followers to receive the same fate: "If they persecuted me, they will also persecute you" (John 15:20; cf. Matt. 10:24–25). One day he will come again, this time in glory and undisguised supremacy (Rev. 19:11–21). But in the meantime, in this overlap of the ages, we who belong to Christ follow him in his pattern of death-unto-resurrection.

---

38 Martin Luther, *The Freedom of a Christian: A New Translation*, trans. Robert Kolb, Crossway Short Classics (Wheaton, IL: Crossway, 2023), 45; Morna D. Hooker, "Interchange in Christ," *JTS* 22, no. 2 (1971): 349–61; Morna D. Hooker, "Interchange in Christ and Ethics," *JSNT* 8, no. 25 (1985): 5–10, 14.

39 See Ortlund, "Power Is Made Perfect in Weakness" 88–94.

Conclusion

IT WOULD BE DIFFICULT to overstate the pathos, raw emotion, and longing with which 2 Corinthians is laced. Yet for all its pastoral earthiness, this letter is not the less theologically rich. Indeed, we have seen that 2 Corinthians makes a distinctive theological contribution to the Bible, in particular through two macro themes under which several theological motifs are subsumed.

Of these two macro themes, one is eschatological and the other is existential—that is, one speaks to where we are in human history while the other is more personally experiential. These are the themes of inaugurated eschatology and strength through weakness. We have seen how pervasive both of these themes are throughout this epistle.

Beneath these two banners are several other important motifs, all of which more or less flow from these banners: Jesus Christ, the Holy Spirit, Satan, friendship, and heaven.

The strategy of this book has been to move through 2 Corinthians, taking these themes in the order in which they surface, resisting the temptation to import notions from systematic theology and probing instead what Paul himself meant by such motifs.

Perhaps no other letter in the New Testament takes its readers so deeply into the heart of what ministry in the new realm, united to a crucified and risen Lord, looks like.

Acknowledgments

I THANK DRS. BRIAN ROSNER AND TOM SCHREINER for inviting me to contribute this volume to this series. Each man is a godly scholar, and it has been an honor working with them. I also thank Justin Taylor, book publisher at Crossway and my friend for over twenty years now, for his counsel and encouragement all the way through this writing project.

Mentioning these three men takes me back to the annual meeting of the Evangelical Theological Society in San Diego in 2019, where the four of us first sat down to dream about this series. I was working for Crossway at the time. It was fun to be there as the series was conceived and now to be able to loop back into the series as a contributor. God ejected me from my Crossway cockpit in summer 2020 and parachuted me into the pastorate. Though I can perceive only a tiny fraction of all that God is doing in my life, I do believe there is a fitting providence in having now spent some years in pastoral ministry before writing this volume on 2 Corinthians. Before I served as a pastor, 2 Corinthians was, for me, true but abstract. This is certainly not to say only pastors can understand this letter. But in a deeper way, I have now begun to understand from the inside what Paul is talking about when he speaks of the death and anguish of the minister through which the Spirit works life and relief for the saints. Only a little. And I'll die one day without fully understanding it. But the message of 2 Corinthians is no longer mainly theoretical to me. And this one letter, more than any other, has kept my heart afloat these early years of ministry. I thank the Lord for the privilege. And I thank Crossway, and Tom and Brian, for being my friends and partners in this project—as well as Chris Cowan, whose deft editorial care gently lifted the book into greater clarity.

This book is dedicated to Dr. Hans Bayer, who listened and counseled patiently as 2 Corinthians began to break open to me in 2003 at Covenant Theological Seminary. He then oversaw my ThM thesis as I gave a year of my life to this letter in 2006. I love him and thank God for him.

I thank also my church family, Naperville Presbyterian Church, for giving me time away each year to write and for praying me through this writing project in the summer of 2022. NPC, I *love* being your pastor. And of course I publicly acknowledge those closest in my heart—my wife, Stacey, and my kids, Zachary, Nathan, Jeremiah, Chloe, and Benjamin—for their love and support. How drab and colorless life would be without you!

The editors and I together offer this book to the church in the spirit of 2 Corinthians 12:19: "It is in the sight of God that we have been speaking in Christ, and all for your upbuilding, beloved."

General Index

Scripture Index

158   SCRIPTURE INDEX

New Testament Theology

The Beginning of the Gospel
A Theology of Mark

PETER ORR

From the Manger to the Throne
A Theology of Luke

BENJAMIN L. GLADD

The Mission of the Triune God
A Theology of Acts

PATRICK SCHREINER

Ministry in the New Realm
A Theology of 2 Corinthians

DANE C. ORTLUND

United to Christ, Walking in the Spirit
A Theology of Ephesians

BENJAMIN L. MERKLE

Hidden with Christ in God
A Theology of Colossians and Philemon

KEVIN W. MCFADDEN

The God Who Judges and Saves
A Theology of 1 Peter and Jude

MATTHEW S. HARMON

The Joy of Hearing
A Theology of the Book of Revelation

THOMAS R. SCHREINER

Edited by Thomas R. Schreiner and Brian S. Rosner, this series presents clear, scholarly overviews of the main theological themes of each book of the New Testament, examining what they reveal about God and his relation to the world in the context of the overarching biblical narrative.

For more information, visit **crossway.org**.